SALMAN RUSHDIE

A BEGINNER'S GUIDE

SALMAN RUSHDIE

A BEGINNER'S GUIDE

ANDREW BLAKE

Series Editors
Rob Abbott & Charlie Bell

Hodder & Stoughton

A MEMBER OF THE HODDER HEADLINE GROUP

Orders: please contact Bookpoint Ltd, 130 Milton Park, Abingdon, Oxon OX14 4SB. Telephone: (44) 01235 827720, Fax: (44) 01235 400500. Lines are open from 9.00–6.00, Monday to Saturday, with a 24-hour message answering service. Email address: orders@bookpoint.co.uk

British Library Cataloguing in Publication Data
A catalogue record for this title is available from The British Library.

ISBN 0 340 80272 3

First published 2001
Impression number 10 9 8 7 6 5 4 3 2 1
Year 2007 2006 2005 2004 2003 2002 2001

Cover photo from Corbis Images.
Typeset by Transet Limited, Coventry, England.
Printed in Great Britain for Hodder & Stoughton Educational, a division of Hodder Headline Plc, 338 Euston Road, London NW1 3BH by Cox & Wyman, Reading, Berks.

CONTENTS

How to use this book

The *Beginner's Guide* series aims to introduce readers to major writers of the past 500 years. It is assumed that readers will begin with little or no knowledge and will want to go on to explore the subject in other ways.

BEGIN READING THE AUTHOR

This book is a companion guide to Rushdie's major works, it is not a substitute for reading the books themselves. It would be useful if you read some of the works in parallel, so that you can put theory into practice. This book is divided into sections. After considering how to approach Rushdie's work and a brief biography, we go on to explore some of his main writings and themes before examining some critical approaches to the author. The survey finishes with suggestions for further reading and possible areas of further study.

HOW TO APPROACH UNFAMILIAR OR DIFFICULT TEXTS

Coming across a new writer may seem daunting, but do not be put off. The trick is to persevere. Much good writing is multi-layered and complex. It is precisely this diversity and complexity which makes literature rewarding and exhilarating.

Literary work often needs to be read more than once, and in different ways. These ways can include: a leisurely and superficial reading to get the main ideas and narrative; a slower more detailed reading focusing on the nuances of the text, concentrating on what appear to be key passages; and reading in a random way, moving back and forth through the text to examine such things as themes, or narrative or characterization. In complex texts it may be necessary to read in short chunks. When it comes to tackling difficult words or concepts it is often enough to guess in context on the first reading, making a more detailed study using a dictionary or book of critical concepts on later reading. If you prefer to look up unusual words as you go along, be careful that you do not disrupt the flow of the text and your concentration.

VOCABULARY

You will see that KEY WORDS and KEY FACTS are set in **bold** text. The words are defined and explained in the GLOSSARY to be found at the back of the book. The facts are explained in the text.

The book is a tool to help you appreciate a key figure in literature. We hope you enjoy reading it and find it useful.

* * * *SUMMARY* * * *

To maximize the use of this book:

- **read the author's work**
- **read it several times in different ways**
- **be open to innovative or unusual forms of writing**
- **persevere.**

Rob Abbott and Charlie Bell
Series Editors

1 Why read Salman Rushdie?

Salman Rushdie is one of the most powerful voices of our time. He is an intensely literary author whose best work is always politically controversial. He raises uncomfortable issues about our identity in a fast-changing world where the certainties of faith in religion or science or literary value are constantly under scrutiny.

Rushdie's novels and other writings connect together to form a cultural history of the twentieth century, offering dazzling insights into the way of life of three continents, and making trenchant political commentaries on the states of Britain, India and Pakistan. But there is far more to Rushdie than historical and political analysis. He is also a dazzling literary technician, writing prose in a bewildering (but internally consistent) range of styles, drawing on a host of influences from classical and modern European, Asian and Latin American literature – and on an equally wide range of aspects of popular culture, from advertising slogans to rock music.

This range of sources and influences is a useful reference point. Many of Rushdie's works have won prestigious literary prizes. But he is not a highbrow author. He clearly enjoys using the popular music and films which are among the sources for his work. But Rushdie goes way beyond the careful **modernism** of writers such as T.S. Eliot or James Joyce, who assembled clever language games from a similar range of sources. Unlike them, Rushdie is willing, even enthusiastic, to inhabit the voices he describes

KEYWORDS

Modernism: a movement which started in the early twentieth century. Writers, artists and musicians broke with the conventions of their art forms, producing work which was characteristically difficult to understand. It often shocked and disturbed audiences.

Postmodernism: in the second half of the twentieth century many artists rejected modernism. They used the traditions of popular culture and high art together, playfully mixing all kinds of sources. This work is usually less disturbing to audiences.

and uses. In fact, if anyone represents that overused word **postmodernism**, it is Salman Rushdie. His work offers a defence of 'literature', but it is also a cheerful commentary on it; his novels are not an attack on popular culture, but a playful acknowledgement of its power to engage and to move us.

It is this playful attitude, beyond even his willingness to offend political elites, which got Rushdie into terrible trouble in the early 1990s. Rushdie was no stranger to controversy. *Shame* and *Midnight's Children* had offended many of their readers in Pakistan and India. But the level of protest was transformed when his novel *The Satanic Verses* was published. It was condemned by Muslims all over the world as a travesty of their deeply held beliefs. Several of his supporters, including publishers and translators of the book, have been killed. This book above all other texts, with its daunting controversy, forces us to ask what *literature* is, and how – or whether – we should defend it.

Rushdie has asked these questions directly. So far, he has survived these traumatic events; he has gone on to write an award-winning novel for children, as well as further novels for adults. He has continued to court publicity through controversy. In a preface to a collection of writing by Indians, Rushdie claimed that the best of all writing in English was now by Indians, and – even more controversially - that it was qualitatively better than writing by Indians in any of the native languages of the Indian subcontinent. Many Indians have characterised this as a betrayal, arguing that Rushdie should somehow be on 'their' side as, two generations after the withdrawal of the British from their former empire, the writers of the subcontinent attempt to find their own voices by discovering or inventing literatures in their own languages.

Of course, he is not on 'their' side. Salman Rushdie is a writer of an earlier moment and of a different place, educated in India and England, and inhabiting the **postcolonial** and **multicultural** world of the Western metropolitan city. But he also writes as an evangelist for the new voices of people who have moved away from the Indian subcontinent, cosmopolitan figures such as Vikram Seth, Meera Syal and Hanif Kureishi. Rushdie's novels prefigured their emergence, and his work acts as a constant point of comparison to theirs; his imagined India, like theirs, has gone beyond the old-fashioned nationalism which desires roots in a particular language and history.

So Rushdie is a commentator on the past and present whose work helps to inaugurate the future of literature by people of South Asian descent and global citizenship. He connects the magical world of the *Thousand and One Nights* with the Bombay of his childhood, and this in turn is connected with the Birmingham evoked by Meera Syal, the London evoked by Hanif Kureishi, or the New Delhi or New York evoked by Vikram Seth. Above all, Rushdie's writings offer us a map, a way of navigating through the strange new world of the postcolonial city and its myriad connections in culture, time and space.

KEYWORDS

Postcolonial: after the European empires dissolved in the second half of the twentieth century, people in the former colonies, and those who had moved round the world as a result of the empires, found new ways of expressing themselves and coming to terms with their pasts.

Multicultural: thanks to the shifting populations of the postcolonial world, many cities are inhabited by groups of people with significantly different religious and cultural systems. They do not simply integrate into one new community but evolve together, sometimes uneasily.

✻ ✻ ✻ *SUMMARY* ✻ ✻ ✻

Rushdie is an exciting writer. His writings:

- make us think about the meaning of 'literature'
- help us to understand the major cultural shifts of the last 50 years
- have influenced many younger writers.

Biography and influences 2

EARLY LIFE AND WRITING

Salman Rushdie was born in 1947, into a prosperous Muslim family in Bombay, India. He was educated at private schools in India, and then in England at Rugby School and Cambridge University, where he studied not literature but history. After spending a while in a fringe drama group, the young Rushdie, by now a British citizen, settled in London, where he had a career as an advertising copywriter. He claims to have invented the slogan 'naughty but nice', which was the catchphrase of an advertisement campaign for cream. This was the first time the world read Rushdie's prose, and it liked what it saw. While working in advertising Rushdie wrote occasional journalism and began to work on fiction. He had one novel rejected, then his first published novel, *Grimus*, appeared in 1975. It was not very successful. But his second novel, *Midnight's Children*, won him the acclaim of the literary world. Published in 1981, this long and ambitious rendering of the emergence of an independent India won the **Booker Prize** in 1984 – a feat the book repeated in 1993 when it was judged the best novel from among the first 25 winners of the competition, and was awarded the 'Booker of Bookers'.

KEYWORD

Booker Prize: one of the most prestigious literary awards in English fiction, the Booker Prize was established in 1969 by Booker McConnell plc. The Booker Trust awards an annual prize for the best published novel in English by a citizen of the UK, the Commonwealth, Eire or Pakistan.

CONTROVERSY

Meanwhile Rushdie had gone on to write *Shame*, a shorter novel set in Pakistan. *Shame* was published in 1983. Although it was also shortlisted for the Booker Prize, this less ambitious (if controversial) novel failed to repeat the previous book's prizewinning success, and perhaps as a result of this comparative failure Rushdie composed another long would-be blockbuster. The result was *The Satanic Verses*, which was published in September 1988, and although it did not win the Booker Prize it won another prestigious award, the Whitbread Prize for that year. However, protests about the book's portrayal of the foundation of Islam led to riots in India, and the book was publicly burned in Bradford in the north of England (where there is a large Muslim community, mainly Pakistani in origin). When, despite these protests, Rushdie did not apologise, and the publishers refused to withdraw the book, a *fatwa*, or sacred command, was pronounced by the Ayatollah Khomeini, the political and spiritual leader of Iran. In this *fatwa* the Ayatollah commanded that *The Satanic Verses* was blasphemous, and that it was the duty of all believers in Islam to hunt its author down and kill him. This call for the assassination of a citizen of the United Kingdom led to the British government's granting of a unique status to Salman Rushdie, who has ever since been under a high level of police protection, living in secrecy and emerging into the public glare only briefly, and always under guard. While he has not been physically harmed, several translators and publishers of the book have been killed and injured, and at least 37 people have so far died from these assassinations and during riots against the book.

A CONTINUING OUTPUT

Rushdie, though deeply affected by these events, did not withdraw from the world, but continued to work as a writer. He published a work for children, *Haroun and the Sea of Stories*, in 1990 (it won a Writers' Guild award), and another full-length adult novel, *The Moor's Last Sigh*, also a Whitbread Prize winner, followed in 1995. Meanwhile he had also published *The Jaguar Smile*, a book about his journey through Nicaragua in Latin America, a short book about the film *The Wizard of Oz*, and a book of collected essays and reviews, *Imaginary Homelands*. Another long and ambitious novel, *The Ground Beneath Her Feet*, was published in 1999. During 2000 it became known that Rushdie had moved from London to New York, though speculation followed that he had almost immediately moved on to Los Angeles, or even back to London. Wherever he is, his life of protected seclusion continues. His most recent novel is the comparatively short *Fury*, published in September 2001.

WHY RUSHDIE WRITES AS HE DOES

An author's life and experiences do not tell us everything we need to know about their work, but in Rushdie's case they offer some of the set of keys we need to understand why Rushdie writes in the way that he does. We need to look at the condition of the subcontinent in which he was born, at the **diaspora** or spread outwards of people from **South Asia** into the rest of the world and at the life of an intellectual in London in the late twentieth century.

KEYWORDS

Diaspora: originally this referred to the spread of the Jewish people round the world. The term is used to refer to any population which has dispersed as a result of imperialism - African and Irish peoples, as well as Asians.

South Asia: India, Pakistan, Bangladesh and Sri Lanka. A more inclusive term than the one formerly used, the 'Indian subcontinent'.

MIDNIGHT'S CHILD

Salman Rushdie was born at a particular, intense, moment of transition. He entered this world in June 1947, two months before the British (who had been among the rulers of the South Asian subcontinent for 300 years) left, and two new independent states, India and Pakistan, were created. Addressing the people of India, Prime Minister Nehru described the magical moment when, at the midnight hour, the new nation was created. *Midnight's Children* re-enacts this moment and the nation's special focus on 'midnight's children' – born as the new states came into existence. This was, however, as the book makes clear, a deeply troubled process. India was set up as a 'secular' state (though dominated numerically by Hindus), while to the east and west were the two halves of Pakistan, an avowedly Muslim state. The division of land along religious lines had been somewhat arbitrary, and tens of millions of people migrated across the country to live among their co-religionists (Rushdie and his parents later moved from Bombay in India to Karachi in Pakistan). Many of these migrants did not make it, killed by religious riots and massacres. Twenty years later there was a civil war between the two halves of Pakistan, which resulted in the creation of a new independent state, Bangladesh. In Kashmir, in the North West of India, the problems of the divided land are still being fought out today. Nehru's pardonable moment of triumph in the creation of the new India was marred, robbed of its joy by this bloodletting – the final symbolic act of this terrible time was the assassination of the leading Indian nationalist, Gandhi, in January 1948. *Midnight's Children* is not a work of pride but of puzzlement: Rushdie's work is consistently suspicious both of religion and of the old-fashioned nationalism which feeds off religious differences. These events of the time of his birth are one of the reasons why.

Another reason is that Rushdie was educated into a culture too cosmopolitan for the simple faiths of nationalism. Speaking several languages, and educated on two continents, Rushdie is part of what has been called 'Indo-Anglian' culture. This phrase refers to people of Indian origin who speak, and write, in English. It reverses the phrase 'Anglo-Indian', which is used for the British in India, and in particular for the people who resulted from mixed marriages between white British and Asian people. Hindi is perhaps the dominant language of India. In a country which boasts dozens of spoken languages, and where more people speak Tamil than any other single language, the key to this dominance is through **Bollywood** films, made in Mumbai (formerly Bombay), which are in Hindi. However, English – the legacy of the British Empire, and the world's most important business language – is very common in India, and it remains the chief language of higher education. It is still commonly used on All-India Radio and in many newspapers and magazines, and there is a thriving tradition of fiction writing in English.

KEY FACT

Bollywood: the mass-market cinema of India is made in Mumbai, the city known to Salman Rushdie as Bombay. Most Bollywood films are action musicals, using fantasy, realism, and a host of Western and Asian traditions and techniques (very like Rushdie's novels).

It is arguable, in fact, that all this fiction writing is part of the family of texts known and taught collectively as 'English literature'. Rushdie was well aware from early childhood of the literatures of his Muslim and, more specifically, Indian inheritance – such as the *Thousand and One Nights* and the great tale of dynastic conflict among the Hindu gods, the *Maharabharata*. He was then exposed, through an English-style schooling, to the work of writers in English such as Shakespeare, Dickens and Joyce. Literature in English had been an important part of the education of the Indian elite in imperial India. It has been argued that 'English literature' was actually invented as a part of the curriculum not in Britain but in India, in response to a notorious claim made in 1835 by the secretary of the East India Company, the historian Lord Macaulay, that one Western text was worth the whole of Indian literature, and that Indians working for the British should learn British culture. That educational tradition remained important in India and Pakistan in the generation after the end of empire – partly because by this time it was no longer possible to claim a local British or English identity for the category. By the end of the nineteenth century English literature was an inclusive label, welcoming non-British writers in English such as the Pole Joseph Conrad, Americans Henry James and T.S. Eliot, and Irish writers such as James Joyce and Samuel Beckett. It was this inclusive literary world order which, in 1912, gave the Nobel Prize for Literature to the Bengali poet and nationalist writer, Rabindranath Tagore.

Rushdie was educated into this world. Furthermore, he was not a peripheral participant: this was a world in which many Indian writers in English were following in the footsteps of those English writers such as Rudyard Kipling and E.M. Forster who had written in and about India. The novelists Mulk Raj Anand and R.K. Narayan were among the pioneers of this Indo-Anglian tradition in which Indian writers, using the English language, discussed the political conditions which helped to make the new independent states. Mulk Raj Anand's novel *Coolie* (published in 1936) is one example of Indian nationalism expressed through Indo-Anglian fiction. *Midnight's Children, Shame, The Satanic Verses, The Moor's Last Sigh* and *The Ground Beneath Her Feet* are all in some ways part of this tradition, so it is perhaps unsurprising that Rushdie has insisted that Indo-Anglian writing is more effective than writing in any of the other languages used in the subcontinent.

THE SOUTH ASIAN DIASPORA

However, while *Midnight's Children, Shame* and *The Moor's Last Sigh* can be seen directly as Indo-Anglian texts, other Rushdie novels like *The Satanic Verses* and *The Ground Beneath Her Feet* are not set principally in India or Pakistan, while *Grimus* and *Fury* hardly mention either country. They are about the ways in which people from the South Asian region have come to inhabit the rest of the world, and the troubled ways in which this diaspora has happened. To understand this more clearly we have to return to Rushdie's early life. At the age of 13 – in 1960 – he went to Rugby School, which is one of the better known of the so-called public schools (they are in fact privately funded). Here his education in the liberal English tradition continued, and he encountered more of the literary works which provide the basis for much of his own work. But he also encountered racism. The British had become an increasingly racist nation during the nineteenth century, as their empire and their domination of the world's industrial production gave them overwhelming global power. They were collectively convinced of their superiority over Europeans, as well as peoples with darker skins from Asia and Africa. Some of the British used Christianity to help them in this project (seeing those from other religions as lacking the true faith). Others used the work of Charles Darwin, the great Victorian theorist of evolution, to bolster their assumptions. A host of scientific investigations seemed to prove that there was a racial hierarchy, with white people at the top. Meanwhile comic and prose literature for boys obsessively repeated the **metanarrative** of white British superiority over all others, whether Zulus in 1891, or Germans in 1918 or 1945. Rushdie, at Rugby, was seen by some of his schoolfellows as an inferior alien, and was treated as such.

KEYWORDS

Metanarrative: an outline story repeated through many other stories. For example, boy meets girl, and they marry in the final chapter, is the metanarrative of most nineteenth-century novels. The characters are called different names, and the detail of places and events are different, but the outline of the story remains the same, whether in Charlotte Brontë's *Jane Eyre* or Charles Dickens's *Little Dorrit.*

By this time, however, British racist assumptions were more defensive. The British Empire was disintegrating, as the financial implications of two world wars – in a nutshell, bankruptcy – forced the British state to retrench and retreat. Meanwhile the partial culling of a generation of young men during the Second World War, together with changes in work expectations in Britain, had led to a demand for certain types of skilled and semi-skilled labour, and at the end of the 1940s a number of industries such as textiles advertised these vacancies in the territories of the former empire. As a result thousands of people from India, Pakistan and the West Indies came to Britain, eager to find the promised work. These were not the privileged and expensively educated few who accompanied Rushdie to the public schools and universities, but poorer people often with unsophisticated expectations. They too were greeted with a mixture of suspicion and hostility, all the greater as the native British population began to realise that Britain was not global top dog any more.

The South Asian diaspora had begun during the nineteenth century. Asians went to many parts of the British Empire – such as Trinidad,

Guyana, South Africa and Uganda – as **indentured labourers**, where they worked in conditions little better than slavery. Their descendants often became wealthy and successful. But their presence was resented by racists in the countries in which they had settled. In 1972 thousands of Asians were expelled from Uganda by the comic-book dictator Idi Amin. Most of them came to England. So by the time Salman Rushdie settled in London in the late 1970s there was a substantial Asian presence there. Many of those who had moved to Britain from Africa were successful middle-class people, and most of them – even the poorer shopkeepers – expected that their children would enter the professions – the law, accountancy or medicine, for example. In a substantial way this happened. But racism in Britain remained and, whether it was expressed in open ways (such as 'paki-bashing', by groups of young white working-class men) or in more subtle ways (such as the refusal of promotion in the middle-class professions), it continued to scar the experience of the Asian British population. We must read Rushdie's representations of British city life with this in mind.

> **KEYWORD**
>
> **Indentured labour:** when slavery was brought to an end, many employers in parts of the British Empire which had relied on slavery turned to Asia, and imported workers who signed contracts, or **indentures**, to work for several years before returning home. Many of them were treated very badly. Many did not return home when their contracts expired, and thus there are large Asian populations in places like Guyana, Trinidad and Kenya.

SALMAN IN LONDON

Nonetheless, we also have to read Rushdie's early career as a success story. Advertising was an upcoming profession when Rushdie joined in the 1970s. Television, which was opened up to advertising in the late 1950s with the advent of a commercial channel, ITV, had increased opportunities for advertisers, and a gradual process of deregulation in broadcasting and the print media brought more opportunities for clever journalists and copywriters.

Rushdie's first professional writing experience was in copywriting, and it is worth speculating that his presence helped to make copywriting what it is today. Advertising copy was once worthy but dull: advertisers told you about their products, and that was about it. Now advertisements use sharp, quick-witted writing, full of punning games which make the reader smile even while they try to sell the advertiser's product. This tongue-in-cheek cleverness has played an important part in the questioning of differences between 'high' and 'popular' culture which produce the style of writing known as postmodernism. Certainly Rushdie's fiction is full of parodied advertising slogans such as this, from *The Moor's Last Sigh*: 'Baby Softo, sing it louder/Softo-pofto talcum powder' (ch. 11).

Thanks both to his liberal education and his experience of racism, Salman Rushdie had left-wing political sympathies. He was typical of the metropolitan intellectuals who were socially and politically formed before the mid-1980s (when there was a right-wing backlash). Though a Muslim by birth, he had lost his faith. So he was at home in a society which was becoming increasingly aware of itself as 'post-Christian'. In other words, many people acknowledged the values shown in Jesus Christ's life, but they did not necessarily acknowledge the divinity of Christ, or the truth of the Gospels as **revelation**. In this world-view the urban intellectual, and the creative artist in particular, had a special significance. The artist was no longer a part of the priesthood, interpreting the word of God to ordinary people through his art (which had been the role of the painter and sculptor Michaelangelo, or the composer J.S. Bach, for example). He was now a creative individual in his own right. Whether a copywriter thinking up clever advertising slogans, a civil servant editing policy documents or a novelist writing fiction, the metropolitan intellectual was a figure of power.

KEYWORD

Revelation: the idea that truth is revealed to a writer by a Divine source. In the Jewish and Christian traditions, the Ten Commandments are an example. In the Muslim faith, it is believed that the truth was revealed to the Prophet Muhammad by the Angel Gabriel.

THE BURDEN OF REPRESENTATION

Rushdie's ability to intervene in public was increased because of his British Asian status. This tendency is sometimes called the 'burden of representation'. In other words, he was expected to speak not as a unique individual but as a representative British Asian in a racist society, a role he often filled in public statements on matters such as policing and immigration policy – explored in the representation of the immigration process in the early chapters of *The Satanic Verses.* However, much of this burden of representation was lifted by the public reception of *The Satanic Verses.* Because of his apparent denial of Islam, and the ways in which Muslims responded to the book, it was simply no longer possible for Rushdie to speak as a public representative of all British Asians and, while his presence diminished because of his enforced hiding, he became in effect just another of the many urban intellectuals clamouring for a hearing. There are many such people: a 1999 employment survey estimated that there were over 33,000 journalists living in London. This may account in part for the subdued response to *The Ground Beneath Her Feet* – seen as just another (good) novel, for all its length, cleverness and ambition,

The burden of representation

because the *fatwa* has reduced Rushdie's status and because the book is principally concerned with the life of the rock musician, not with Indian or diasporic identity. Having moved through the troubled politics of multiculturalism, Rushdie's work has focused elsewhere, though *Fury*, chiefly set in New York, does not ignore these difficult questions.

RUSHDIE'S INFLUENCE

We will end this chapter by briefly mentioning the ways in which the next generation of writers has developed aspects of Rushdie's agenda. Rushdie is no longer a lone postcolonial voice within British fiction. The Booker Prize has now been awarded to several other non-white writers, including the Indian, Arundhati Roy, whose *The God of Small Things* (winner in 1997) is clearly and positively influenced by Rushdie. Zadie Smith's *White Teeth*, focusing on a British family of Pakistani origin, was one of the most widely praised novels of 2000. The work of Indian-born Vikram Seth includes matters beyond ethnicity, as in his New York-based novel *Equal Music*, which makes little reference to the India he had explored in *A Suitable Boy*. Hanif Kureishi is a British-born Asian whose film scripts, short stories and novels have persistently dealt with the contradictions of multiple identity; his novel *The Black Album* (1994) and the 1998 short story (which was subsequently filmed), *My Son the Fanatic*, also deal specifically with the *fatwa* on *The Satanic Verses* and its legacy to British Asians. But Kureishi, like Seth, has also gone beyond the problem of ethnicity; *Intimacy* (which was published in 1999 and filmed for 2001 release), a rawly felt semi-autobiographical exploration of the politics of relationships, takes the fact of different skin colours for granted, and leaves it at that.

Meanwhile a new generation of British Asians, younger than Kureishi, has come to notice, and their success has moved British Asian culture into the mainstream. The work of Talvin Singh, Nitin Sawhney and the bands Cornershop and Asian Dub Foundation have all been shortlisted for the Mercury Prize, the British music scene's equivalent of the Booker Prize. In television, the all-Asian comedy sketch show *Goodness Gracious Me* has been broadcast on prime time, and one of its writers, Meera Syal, has also written an influential film (*Bhaji on the Beach*) and become a successful novelist – the autobiographical *Anita and Me* and the more distanced *Life isn't all Ha Ha Hee Hee* are both bestsellers. Rushdie himself notes the new confidence of Asian actors in Britain in the preface to his screenplay adaptation of *Midnight's Children*: 'At the time of the original publication of *Midnight's Children*, there would have been very few such actors to choose from. One generation later, we were able to audition a diverse and multitalented throng' (ch. 9). It would be an exaggeration to say that Rushdie was personally responsible for all this, but the pioneering success of his work helped to make the world more receptive for work by people from the Asian diaspora. The rest of this book will explain why his work is so successful.

* * * SUMMARY * * *

- **Rushdie has lived in India and England – he is part of the 'South Asian diaspora'.**
- **His English education brought him into contact with racism.**
- **His success made him a voice for Asians in Britain.**
- **He worked in advertising before becoming a novelist.**
- **He is a 'metropolitan intellectual'.**

Major works (1): The fiction 3

Salman Rushdie is one of the most accomplished writers of fiction at work today, and the next two chapters aim to show how and why. This chapter looks at each novel and the short stories. The next chapter will explore in more detail some of the ways in which Rushdie's writing style, his ideas and influences, and the themes elaborated in his texts combine to produce his particular authorial voice.

We need to notice, first, that Rushdie's writing career had two beginnings. His first novel, *Grimus*, hardly emerged from the sea of stories which are published each year. It was only with the publication of *Midnight's Children* that the world began to realise that here was a new and powerful voice in fiction. So in some ways the proper place to start a survey of the novels would be *Midnight's Children*. However, *Grimus* is important to the development of Rushdie's writing. He has added to its experimental blend of storytelling techniques, but they remain the basis for his work. Imagine a world produced by a blend of folk tales and science fiction stories, told by a narrator who knows a great deal of the history and literatures of the world. Imagine a world in which time as we know it stands still, and in which the chief participants of the story are manipulated by a largely unseen character. Imagine a story whose chief purpose is to bring itself and its world to an end. This is the world of *Grimus*.

GRIMUS

We meet Virgil Jones and Dolores O'Toole descending a cliff path to the beach of the island they inhabit. At first the only strange thing about this is the language of the opening chapter, which is derived from the wordplay of James Joyce – a trick which is repeated later in the book, whenever Jones is allowed a **soliloquy**. Once we are on the beach the prose becomes more simple, but the story becomes more strange.

KEYWORD

Soliloquy: a speech given out loud by an individual, not addressed directly to any listener who might be present. A device used in drama and fiction to allow an audience to hear what a character is thinking.

Flapping Eagle has landed. In a chapter of first-person narrative (written without the Joycean wordplay), Flapping Eagle reveals that he is a North American 'Indian' who looks 34 but is in fact 440 years old: he has become to all intents and purposes immortal thanks to drinking a yellow fluid given to him by his sister (and lover), Bird-Dog. Flapping Eagle has come to Calf Island to try to find his sister and end his immortality. Calf Island, it turns out, is in a parallel slice of spacetime to earth, a place where those who have become immortal go to be with their own kind. It's an amalgam of fantasy, folk and science fiction: the island is a mythical place made up of elements from the world's stories – including Kaf mountain, the mountain of ever-changing birds of Arabian folklore, and Yggdrassil, the world ash-tree of Norse mythology. The island is held in its place thanks to the thoughts and energies of a creature from another planet, a Gorf, a member of an immobile but multidimensional rock-formed alien species devoted to the pursuit of mind games. Grimus, a human, has made a machine which links the island to the many dimensions inhabited by the Gorfs. Jones and Eagle go to K, a small town inhabited by immortalised humans who pass the time by role-playing characters such as hunter, bar keeper, pimp, whore, magistrate, philosopher and so on. The plot advances by a series of violent and/or sexual confrontations, through which Eagle finally meets Grimus, destroys the machines which have enabled humans to become immortal and to take part in the Gorf game, and brings Calf Island's existence to an end.

This rich mix of myth and legend, science fiction and philosophy surrounds a central question which occurs throughout Rushdie's writing. It is the question of identity. Who are we; how do we know, and what can we do about it to change the circumstances in which we have our being? In *Grimus* – and in all his work, but in *Haroun and the Sea of Stories*, *The Satanic Verses* and *The Moor's Last Sigh* in particular

– these questions are addressed through an investigation into forms of writing. In these works Rushdie explores his own literary heritage, and reworks it in ways which continually emphasise that *we are written* – all our identities are fluidly mixed into the 'sea of stories'. As seas ebb, flow and change, so do those stories and the ways in which we can interpret them. Well before the controversy over *The Satanic Verses*, Rushdie was exploring the effects of writing on identity.

Grimus, then, started several strands in Rushdie's work. But *Grimus* is fantasy, certainly without any clear political **satire**. The controversy over *The Satanic Verses* arose partly because Rushdie was by this time perceived as a writer of novels with more directly political intentions. He had already offended many powerful people through his next two novels, *Midnight's Children* and *Shame*. These two books are also concerned with ways of writing, with the blending of genres such as fantasy and folk tale, and with the effects of writing on identity; but they are also in some ways 'realist' novels, set not in the completely parallel timespace of *Grimus* but in the twentieth century, and in particular, identifiable times and places. They deal with real political events and with some of the real historical actors in those events.

KEYWORDS

Satire: a representation of public figures, or social trends, which exaggerates their worst features. Usually political, as well as comic, in intention.

Oral storytelling: traditions in which stories are learned and transmitted by the spoken word rather than through writing.

MIDNIGHT'S CHILDREN

Midnight's Children is written on a very grand scale. The UK paperback edition has 463 pages, as opposed to the 253 pages of *Grimus*. The book is quite deliberately epic, and it engages with an epic moment in history – the political and cultural transformations which followed the end of British rule in India. But it is just as concerned as *Grimus* with the contradictory forces which produce the identity of the individual – and the tale weaves the personal, and the magical, with the political. It is all wrapped up in a narrative which owes a great deal to the **oral storytelling** traditions of India. In its constant, almost casual juxtaposition of the real with the fantastic, it also draws heavily from the plots and storytelling techniques used by the Bollywood cinema industry. The narrator, Saleem Sinai, a worker in a pickle factory, tells his story to a fellow-worker, Padma (who acts as a slightly sceptical 'listener' to Saleem's tale on behalf of the reader, asking him to explain the more obscure parts of the story). Saleem was born in Bombay at midnight on 15 August 1947, just as the new state of India came into existence; but Saleem's narrative begins 30 years earlier, with his grandfather, the European-educated doctor Aadam Aziz, who loses his Muslim faith, gains a wife, then witnesses a turning point in the Anglo-Indian relationship, the Amritsar Massacre of 1926. When General Dyer ordered his troops to fire on an unarmed crowd, 1,650 people were killed or injured (in the aftermath Rabindranath Tagore returned his Nobel Prize). Aadam Aziz has three daughters, the second of whom, Amina, marries Ahmed Sinai and becomes the narrator's mother, her pregnancy taking place during the increasingly turbulent communal disturbances which preceded the partition of the subcontinent.

KEY FACT

India was set up as a 'secular' state not to deny religious belief, but to try to preserve all the different faith communities (and language groups) in the country, and to protect their interests. The word **communal** refers to the faith communities.

KEYWORD

Magic realism: a technique used first by a number of Latin American writers which describes extraordinary people and events as if they were part of normal, everyday reality.

The family moves into a European-style Bombay house recently vacated by an Englishman, Sir William Methwold. When our midnight's child is born, the nurse swaps Amina's baby with another, born to a poor woman who was formerly Methwold's servant; he has a big nose like his grandfather's, but also blue eyes. This is Saleem. The narrative explores the development of family relations, before the world of **magic realism** makes its first appearance in the novel. Saleem's grotesquely large nose begins to sing, and he hears voices. In Saleem's own words, he becomes a radio, able both to receive and to broadcast, and he becomes the voice of the surviving midnight's children, all of whom have magical powers of some sort. But these children, though they meet together in Saleem's mind, do not make a collective movement, and Saleem's hopes for the country's transformation are dashed. When Saleem's finger is damaged by school bullies a blood test revels the truth of his parenthood. He is in fact Methwold's son; an Anglo-Indian. We follow Saleem's life as his grandfather rediscovers his Muslim faith and the family move to Pakistan; eventually, having lost his telepathic powers but gained an acute sense of smell, he takes part in the Pakistani civil war which produced the new state of Bangladesh. By this time he has begun to age (and disintegrate physically) faster than normal.

For a while Saleem lives in the old city centre of Delhi. Here a son is born, also at midnight, during the state of emergency imposed by Prime Minister Mrs Indira Gandhi in 1972. Mrs Gandhi is portrayed as the incarnation of the worst aspects of the Hindu goddess Kali (the goddess who is caricatured in Steven Spielberg's film *Indiana Jones and the Temple of Doom*). Mrs Gandhi's government tortures Saleem, forcing him to name the rest of the children, and finally castrates him. But in a fantastic episode which we are meant to take as an extended **metaphor** for Indian history and spirituality as a whole, Saleem is given a son. Aadam Sinai is born to two of his fellow midnight's children, including Shiva, the baby he was changed for. The parents are named after Hindu deities Shiva and Parvati, who were the parents of the elephant-headed Hindu god Ganesh. But the Muslim-born Saleem acts as his father. Saleem ends his narrative as a worker in a Bombay pickle factory, telling his story to the sympathetic but quizzical Padma, and optimistic that his 'son', Aadam Sinai, will be able to channel the magic powers he has inherited more profitably than Saleem has managed.

KEYWORD

Metaphor: a form of comparison using a word or idea which is not literally applicable to what the writer is describing, in order to illustrate shared characteristics.

Grimus is interesting, clever, intriguing; but *Midnight's Children* is an extraordinary novel. Adding autobiographical, historical and political elements to the previous mixture of legend, fantasy fiction and literary cleverness, this book is almost shockingly inventive. While it pleased most critics, some of its readers were shocked, and did not like the effect. Indeed, the family of Mrs Gandhi were first publicly critical of the author, and then sued him for libel. One brief episode from the book was removed. Having apologised, Rushdie proceeded to repeat the exercise, and then some, with his next and most deliberately political novel, *Shame*.

SHAME

This shorter novel opens with a fairytale event to match Saleem's imaginary fatherhood: a shared pregnancy, through which Omar Khayyam Shakil is born, magically, to three sisters, all of whom share the role of mother, but who withdraw from all contact with the world outside. Then a first-person narrator takes us into the world of Pakistani high politics: corruption, nepotism and dictatorship. This occasional narrator, who does not identify himself directly, seems to be Salman Rushdie. Moving beyond the autobiographical hints and parallels of *Midnight's Children*, the novel contains personally expressed political opinion: this is the voice of a writer who has gained confidence with success and now wishes to make his fiction work in the wider world. 'I tell myself this will be a novel of leave-taking' of the East, he informs us (p. 2). But he is also cautious and aware of the possibilities that his work will be ignored or vilified by those whom it treats. Through this authorial voice we learn that the novel is about a country which is very like Pakistan, but that it is not quite a realist novel; it is written 'at a slight angle to reality' (p. 2). In other words the narrator is claiming that *Shame* is not a direct account of the real Pakistan which was ruled over first by the corrupt civilian, Zulfikar Ali Bhutto, and then by the military dictator, General Zia ul-Haq. The narrator thus formally denies, but also *at the same time* invites, the reader to identify his character Iskander Harappa with Bhutto, and his

General Raza Hyder with General Zia ul-Haq. The parallels between the states over which these two and their families preside are not exact, but the similarities are striking, and every so often the first-person narrator returns to point them out, all the while insisting that his is a work of fiction.

Indeed, the narrator insists, it is a fable or fairytale. We meet once again, as in *Grimus*, the mountain of Kaf, and the Norse world ash-tree Yggdrassil, as the narrator emphasises the story's connections with literature and myth. The book opens and closes with fantastic events, and narrated alongside the realist story of the rise and interaction of the dynasties which govern this parallel-Pakistan (whose family trees are drawn for us at the beginning of the book) is the story of Sufiya Zinobia, a woman whose mental capacities grow more slowly than her body, and who embodies and expresses shame through a series of violently destructive outbursts. Sufiya, clearly intended as a metaphor for Pakistan as a whole, has the power to destroy those who shame her and the country in which she lives, and she presides over the final ruin of the dynasties which have run the country.

Many of the Pakistanis who read *Shame* saw the novel as a political tract. They refused to believe the narrator's claims about the fabulous nature of the tale, and they criticised Rushdie for painting a partial, outsider's picture of their country. As with *Midnight's Children*, there was a mounting critical response from South Asia as a whole, which saw Rushdie as a stateless voice more representative of the West's view of the world than the Asian view. Other critics registered disappointment with the scale of the book. It was shortlisted for the Booker Prize but did not win.

Perhaps because of this comparative failure, and the critical voices which had commented on the novel, Salman Rushdie's next novel was a return to the epic. It was principally about the problem of identity among those who had moved to countries with very different world-views, and who tried to reconcile the differences they had encountered within themselves. One of the first-person narrative moments of *Shame* tells us that the novel had first been conceived while Rushdie was thinking about the death of a young Muslim woman in London (whose family had killed her as a matter of 'honour'), and that as he first thought of it the book would have addressed the problems of identity confronted by individuals, families and communities which have settled outside their homelands. Rushdie now began to explore this problem, exploring the crisis of identity suffered by two South Asian men who experience London in the 1980s.

THE SATANIC VERSES

The surreal opening of *The Satanic Verses*

The novel opens with a surreal episode in which Bollywood actor Gibreel Farishta and voice-over artist Saladin Chamcha fall from an aircraft, landing miraculously alive on the beach at Dover. Chamcha is picked up and treated as a dangerous illegal immigrant, subject to the tyrannical British police who treat immigrants as monsters, not people.

The result of this enormous difference of perception on the people concerned is **schizophrenia** – they become individuals with multiple identities. Sure enough, Chamcha apparently begins to turn into a goat-like devil, while Farishta thinks of himself as an angel. Written in the late 1980s, the novel comments repeatedly and critically on Prime Minister Mrs Margaret Thatcher's London, with its mix of private wealth and decaying public infrastructure, and its constantly strained race relations. In a witty fantasy episode Gibreel Farishta, convinced that he has been transformed into an angel flying over London, imagines that he can transform it into a tropical city, and he describes the positive changes this would make on the cold, unimaginative and unwelcoming white population. The final part of the novel sees both protagonists back in human form in Bombay, though only one of them has survived his transformative experiences by the end.

KEYWORD

Schizophrenia: a mental disease in which thoughts and actions are disconnected. Schizophrenics often experience multiple personalities – they think of themselves as several different people – or they experience inner voices, which they do not think are their own, telling them what to do.

Unfortunately for Rushdie, this outline does not represent the book which his opponents seemed to read. Though most of *The Satanic Verses* is set in London, it contains many subplots set in the Indian subcontinent, and many more episodes set in the minds of the protagonists (who are indeed schizophrenic, mentally unhinged by the enormous problems of adjusting to life in an often hostile Western society). In one of these episodes, in a lightly disguised parallel to the accepted account, Gibreel Farishta re-imagines the founding of the Islamic religion, and the ways in which the holy book of Islam, the Qur'an, was dictated to the Prophet Muhammad by Divine revelation. The episode of the Satanic Verses is a story which was not invented by Rushdie. It was current soon after the establishment of Islam, though most Islamic scholars have discounted it as a historical event. In this story some verses were given by Satan, impersonating the angel

(Gibreel, or Gabriel) who dictated the rest of the work. They suggested that three female deities should be worshipped alongside the one god, Allah. This impersonation was discovered and the verses were expunged from the book. Rushdie plays with history and the nature of writing and identity here, as he does elsewhere in his work, and the passages on the Satanic Verses and the founding of Islam are not offered as a straightforward history: the Prophet is called Mahound, and the holy city of Jahilia is not Mecca. However, these passages were interpreted as genuine attempts to insult Islam by people whom he had already offended both as South Asians and as Muslims, and who were therefore all the readier to take offence at his representations of the Prophet's life and times. It did not help Rushdie's cause that 'Mahound' had been a medieval European insult for the Prophet Muhammad. Many Muslims think that the episode of the Satanic Verses is also a Western invention.

HAROUN AND THE SEA OF STORIES

As we know, the furore which followed the publication of *The Satanic Verses* resulted in the permanent internal exile of Salman Rushdie. Rushdie's response as a writer was to write a children's book. Wonderful as *Haroun and the Sea of Stories* is, this may seem a bizarre, even cowardly option, a retreat back to pure fantasy from the political world of the previous three fictions. In fact *Haroun*, and the following novel, *The Moor's Last Sigh*, are part of Rushdie's defence of the arts of writing; but they are also part of the literary strand in his work which was first explored in *Grimus* and which is also present in the mythological aspects of the other novels. These texts defend the arts of writing, and they defend Rushdie as a writer.

The inspiration for *Haroun and the Sea of Stories* had been with Rushdie for a long time. In his short appreciation of the film, *The Wizard of Oz*, published in 1992, Rushdie tells us that he had written his very first story after he had seen the film, as a 10-year-old boy. He had interpreted this magical story through Indian eyes used to such fantasies in the Bombay cinema. He had tried in writing *Haroun and the Sea of Stories* to capture this magic, of a cinematic sense of motion and adventure made for both adults and children.

Haroun and the Sea of Stories tells of Rashid Khalifa and his son Haroun (they are named after Caliph Haroun al-Rashid, the legendary instigator of the *Thousand and One Nights*). Rashid's wife walks out on him, whereon he loses his magical gift of storytelling. In despair, he cancels the subscription which gives him access to the Sea of Stories, an ocean which contains myriad versions of all the stories that have been and will be told in the world. Haroun journeys with a series of magical creatures, Iff the genie and Mali the water-gardener, and a superlatively clever machine, Butt the Hoopoe, to the Sea of Stories and Gup City, from which the subscriptions are run. They confront the corruption which is endangering them, defeat the evil powers which wish to destroy all stories and restore Rashid's ability to tell his tales, at which point his wife returns and family order is restored – just in time for Haroun's birthday. Incidentally, universal light is brought to the moon which harbours the Ocean of the Sea of Stories, and a prince and princess are reunited – in the telling Rushdie has a great deal of fun with his usual sources, Indian and English words and stories, films, books and popular music (especially Beatles' songs).

It is possible to read this charming and witty story as simply that. But it is also a political response to his Muslim critics. The Islamic fundamentalists who had burned his book without reading it are portrayed here. Khattam-Shud, the evil character who tries to poison the Sea of Stories, also wishes to impose universal darkness, and he achieves conformity among his followers by forbidding them from speaking. Insisting both that his fiction was just that, and that those who wish to destroy storytelling are evil, Rushdie aimed a stout, if well disguised, blow against his persecutors.

EAST, WEST

East, West, published three years after *Haroun*, is a collection of short stories which explore the cultural and political problems of a world in which the traveller, the migrant, indeed almost anyone living in the postimperial world of the later twentieth century, all have to come to terms with seeing, and being seen as, **the Other**. At the heart of the collection is 'Christopher Columbus and Queen Isabella of Spain consummate their relationship (Santa Fé, AD 1492)', an exploration of the crucial moment of the beginning of Western imperialism – 1492 was the year in which the Moors and Jews were expelled from Spain, while Columbus moved West to 'discover' the Americas for Europe. The final story, 'The Courter', is set among a family which moves from Bombay to London during the 1960s. The first-person narrator tells of the family servant, certainly-Mary, her refusal to acclimatise, and her eventual return to Bombay, while the narrator becomes part of a multicultural London encountering racist hostility but also enjoying contact with Western popular culture (rock music, television cartoon *The Flintstones* and professional football) and moving towards British citizenship – just as Rushdie himself had done when in Britain as a schoolboy in the 1960s. At the end of *East, West* Rushdie seems to be asserting his own identity once more.

> **KEYWORD**
>
> **The Other:** a term to help us understand that we define ourselves by defining what or who we are not. Derived from psychoanalysis, the term has become important in postcolonial theory.

THE MOOR'S LAST SIGH

It is perhaps surprising, then, that the next novel, *The Moor's Last Sigh*, was set almost entirely in India; but, like its predecessors, this is a postcolonial and postmodern fiction, exploring the multitudinous and almost irreconcilable ethnic and communal differences within India. *The Moor's Last Sigh* was another prizewinner (awarded the Whitbread Novel of the Year for 1995), and it is another substantial book: the UK paperback runs to 423 pages. The first-person narrator, Moraes Zogoiby, imprisoned and dying in a remote Spanish village, writes the story of his family. The often forgotten Jewish and Christian heritages of India come together in the Zogoiby family, who have moved to Bombay from Goa (the small former Portuguese colony on the west coast of India, which became part of the Indian state only in 1963). Here they make pickles – a culinary definition of Indianness which is also important to *Midnight's Children* and to Arundhati Roy's *The God of Small Things*, and one which arguably transcends any ethnic or religious peculiarities. Moraes Zogoiby (the 'Moor' of the title) is born in 1957. He has the unusual attributes of being without fingers on his right hand, and of living at twice the normal speed, having the body of a 20-year-old at age 10 and so on.

Like Saleem Sinai, the narrator tracks back to times before his birth, telling us about the contradictory ways in which the family responded to the end of British rule and the political changes thereafter, including an engagement with the local and business politics of Bombay itself (though there is less of the waspish commentary on the characters and events depicted here than we find in *Shame* or *Midnight's Children*, these passages are very political). Indian history and the narrator's development are portrayed through descriptions of his mother Aurora's paintings. Borrowing a technique from writers such as Balzac and Trollope, Rushdie reintroduces his own fictional characters into this world, emphasising the extended realism of his Bombay: Saleem Sinai's 'son' Aadam Sinai reappears, by now a frightful **yuppie**. Bombay is arguably the hero of the story, a place which resonates with its Anglo-Portuguese origins and hybrid growth thereafter, the mix of peoples and opportunities within its bounds; but at the end, Bombay fails the narrator (ch. 18) because it does not contain his roots. As a descendant of the Cochin Jews who had been expelled from Spain at the same time as the Moors, it is appropriate that his end, and the end of the novel, is set in the former

KEYWORD

Yuppie: literally 'young, upwardly mobile professional person'. The term was used satirically to describe the aggressive and selfish people who were successful in the 1980s.

Moorish state of Andalusia. The story of the deformed Moor's birth and growth is less political than personal. His relationship with his mother, and the freakish young man's search for real love beyond that twisted parental bond, forms the central focus of a book which is long and ambitious, though not as epic in scope as *Midnight's Children* or *The Satanic Verses.*

THE GROUND BENEATH HER FEET

Ambition and scope were redoubled for Rushdie's next novel (though it was not shortlisted for the Booker Prize). Far more than *Shame*, where the attempt to build a parallel-world Pakistan is deliberately paper-thin, *The Ground Beneath Her Feet* sets out to write an alternative history, based on **classical mythology**. The mythological basis to the novel is a version of the legend of Orpheus and Eurydice, the story of obsessive love in which the great minstrel Orpheus tries to rescue his dead lover, bringing her from the Underworld back to ours, and only failing at the last minute by looking back to see whether she is following him. The novel's parallel history revolves around the proposition that the Indian subcontinent produced a distinctive contribution to rock music in the 1960s and thereafter. In order to show how this might have happened, in the first third of the book Rushdie inscribes another first-person experiential history of Bombay in the mid-twentieth century. As he had done in *The Moor's Last Sigh*, Rushdie reintroduces previous characters: Aurora Zogoiby is mentioned several times, while Sir William Methwold has a substantial role. Meanwhile the 'real', including both politics and the rock world, is distorted somewhat in the telling, to emphasise the parallel nature of Rushdie's magic realism. President Kennedy is not killed in Dallas in 1963, and the British join the Americans in the Vietnam War. John Lennon (and not Mick Jagger) sings 'Satisfaction', Carly Simon rather than Paul Simon is credited with 'Bridge over Troubled Water' and the punk movement is relabelled 'runt'.

> **KEYWORD**
>
> **Classical mythology:** the set of myths and legends dealing with the gods and goddesses of ancient Greece and Rome.

The principal protagonists in this parallel world are the narrator, photographer Umeed 'Rai' Merchant and the emerging rock stars Ormus Cama and Vina Apsara. Ormus Cama is from a Bombay family of the Parsi religion, with an Anglophile father and a mother who retires to England on her husband's death and marries Sir William Methwold. Cama is extravagantly musically gifted. Vina Apsara is a great singer from a mixed, indeed mixed-up, background. With a French mother and an Indian father who has come out as gay, brought up in the Midwestern USA in an adoptive family all of whom are killed when she is 12, she is then brought to India to live in the family of a corrupt businessman. Here she meets and falls for Ormus Cama (it is mutual, though seldom consummated until marriage), while Umeed falls for her, spending much of the rest of the novel in respectful pursuit – and occasional, sexual, attainment – of his beloved.

The remaining two-thirds of the novel move away from the fast-modernising corruption of Bombay, and into the global world of the music business, its legal disputes and journalistic ancillaries. London and then New York become the urban backgrounds for Rushdie's exploration of genius and obsession. Ormus Cama is hurt in a car crash, and thereafter develops apocalyptic thoughts about parallel worlds exploding into his own, writing an album of songs about earthquakes. Vina dies in just such an earthquake, and Ormus responds by reinventing their band, VTO, with a lookalike singer. But at the end of the novel a woman with Vina's appearance shoots Ormus, then disappears, and it seems that the Orpheus legend has been reversed: both protagonists will be together in the underworld.

FURY

The much shorter *Fury*, published in September 2001, also uses classical mythology – the story of the three Furies, snake-haired goddesses who avenged crime – in an exploration of male mid-life crisis. The book centres around Professor Malik Solanka, a self-made millionaire. He leaves his wife, Eleanor, and Asmaan, his son, in England after a moment of extreme anger and moves to New York.

Here he tries to explore his anger through a series of new relationships. Unusually for Rushdie the past is not the centre of the investigation. Bombay and London are part of the background of a story which continually reminds us that it is set not in a parallel world – as in *Shame* or *The Ground Beneath Her Feet* – but in New York in the year 2000. The American presidential election which brought George W. Bush to power is in full swing, *Buffy the Vampire Slayer* is on television and the sporting world is dominated by the exploits of golfer Tiger Woods.

As Malik Solanka tries to heal himself of the anger which has built up within him he meets and befriends people, tells them parts of his story and learns theirs. We meet wealthy young socialites who turn out to be serial killers. Then we come across a group of nerdy computer-game developers led by Mila, a young woman, who help Solanka to build a new business selling puppets based on a science fiction story. Finally there is Neela Mahendra, an ultra-beautiful young woman who is devoted to the political cause of a group of former indentured labourers on a South Pacific island strongly resembling Fiji, but which Rushdie, echoing Swift, calls Lilliput-Blefescu. In a moment of confrontation, Eleanor, Mila and Neela act as the Furies, threatening Malik's life; he admits his guilt, loses his anger and returns to London to try to rebuild a relationship with his son.

The tranquil end to *Fury*

An exploration of history and myth, fact and fiction, the traditions of folklore and literature, and a personal defence of the writer's craft: these are the characteristics of Salman Rushdie's fictional output. They are all to be found in each of his fictions, where they are bound together with an increasing mastery of that craft. From *Grimus* to *Fury*, Rushdie's deployment of the elements in his writing becomes increasingly confident and characteristic. The next chapter explores some of the ways in which the writing style and thematic interests combine to form Salman Rushdie's unique authorial voice.

* * * *SUMMARY* * * *

- **Read these books, preferably several times!**
- ***Grimus* plays with folk tale, myth and science fiction.**
- ***Midnight's Children* and *Shame* are about the South Asian subcontinent in the twentieth century, but they also play with myth and fantasy.**
- ***The Satanic Verses* has more about South Asians in the West than in India or Pakistan.**
- ***Haroun and the Sea of Stories* is a magical children's adventure, but it is also a defence of the creative writer.**
- ***The Moor's Last Sigh* explores the interconnectedness of people and culture through history.**
- ***The Ground Beneath Her Feet* retells the myth of Orpheus and Eurydice from an Indian viewpoint.**
- ***Fury* juxtaposes myth and science fiction in the modern world.**

4 The major themes

This chapter will draw out the common themes of the novels, concentrating on Salman Rushdie's attempt to construct a *postcolonial voice*. While he uses English for all his major published work, and while much of the novels' source material is from 'English literature', Rushdie consistently adopts accents, dialects, languages and literatures from elsewhere, and he then revisits the history of South Asia within this new voice. The result is a *style* – in other words, we can quickly recognise a piece of writing by Rushdie thanks to these techniques. Because this style is used consistently, we can also claim that it is part of the author's identity. But the style is also an *idea*. Salman Rushdie is a self-consciously postcolonial and postmodern writer, and he is also self-consciously political. His work adds up to a statement about the political importance of open and flexible cultural change in a world in which culture is too often seen as belonging to closed political and economic systems. The novels' political commentaries, their explorations of the limits of reality and the ways in which literature and popular culture intertwine – which are the major themes of the fiction – are all aspects of this basic claim.

THE BOUNDARIES OF THE TEXT

Salman Rushdie's fictional output is undoubtedly literature. His work refers constantly to popular culture, but, apart from *Haroun and the Sea of Stories*, it is not popular fiction. Long as they are, books like *Midnight's Children* cannot be packaged as 'airport novels'. Some of Rushdie's work is quite difficult to read, and all of it is complex. At the heart of this complexity is the way in which Rushdie draws on existing literature, using models and methods from the literatures of most of the world to weave his own voice. This is partly done by allusion and quotation, but partly by the technique called **pastiche**: the opening pages of *Grimus*, for example, owe a great deal to James Joyce's clever use of puns and original word combinations.

KEYWORD

Pastiche: a copy not of a work but of a style or technique, which tries to mimic the original as closely as possible.

Here is a passage from *Shame* which borrows an earlier technique:

> But suppose this were a realistic novel! Just think what else I might have to put in. The business, for instance, of the illegal installation, by the inhabitants of 'defence', of covert, subterranean water pumps that steal water from their neighbours' mains – so that you can always tell the people with the most pull by the greenness of their lawns (such clues are not confined to the cantonment of Q.). – And would I also have to describe the Sind Club in Karachi, where there is still a sign reading 'Women and Dogs not Allowed Beyond This Point'? Or to analyse the subtle logic of an industrial programme that builds nuclear reactors but cannot develop a refrigerator? O dear – and the school text-books which say 'England is not an agricultural country', and the teacher who once docked two marks from my youngest sister's geography essay because it differed at two points from the exact wording of this same text-book … how awkward, dear reader, all this could turn out to be. (ch. 4)

We are drawn in through this courteous tone to engage with the book as if we were in dialogue with the self-proclaimed narrator. This narrator confesses to us that he is writing fiction, indeed fantasy, but also tells us what the 'real' alternatives are. This technique involves us as readers in giving our consent to the illusion, and it simultaneously reminds us of the ways in which fiction – a conscious effort by the writer to invent characters and events – represents the real world. These paradoxical means of presenting the real are not by any means Rushdie's own discovery. Compare that passage in *Shame* with these words:

> I know that the tune I am piping is a very mild one (although there are some terrific chapters coming presently) and must beg the good-natured reader to remember that we are only discoursing at present

> about a stock-broker's family in Russell Square, who are taking walks, or luncheon, or dinner, or talking and making love as people do in common life, and without a single passionate and wonderful incident to mark the progress of their loves. The argument stands thus – Osborne, in love with Amelia, has asked an old friend to dinner and to Vauxhall – Jos Sedley is in love with Rebecca. Will he marry her? That is the great subject now in hand. (W.M. Thackeray, *Vanity Fair*, 1848; edition used published by Collins, 1954, p.60)

Thus wrote W.M. Thackeray in his novel *Vanity Fair*, telling us that his fiction is about ordinary people, not heroes – just as Rushdie does, he confesses, with the same sense of dialogue with the reader, that his invented tale is about real life. *Vanity Fair* was first published in 1848, at the same time as Charlotte Brontë's *Jane Eyre* and Charles Dickens's *Dombey and Son.* The narrator's passages in *Shame* echo that great moment of 'English literature'. When he writes like Thackeray, Brontë, or Dickens, Rushdie is very confidently placing himself in that tradition and its comfortable relationship with the imagined reader.

But *Shame* is not 'a realist novel', and neither are any of Rushdie's other novels. Rushdie also, and equally confidently, distances himself from that very English tradition: he is not continuing it, but modifying it according to his own specifications. *Grimus* is a fantasy novel, drawing from the world's folk myths and from science fiction alike; it is not *particularly* influenced by the histories and cultural traditions of the Indian subcontinent. But in all the fiction after *Grimus*, Rushdie writes as an Indo-Anglian, educated in schools based on British schools, and then in the British education system itself, but with a background in all the varieties of literary culture open to the Indian subcontinent. He constantly refers to and uses Other literatures, weaving them into the personal version of English which he has constructed. The Arabian text *The Thousand and One Nights*, the sequence of stories told by Scheherezade to Caliph Haroun al-Rashid, which weaves these stories within the longer story of Scheherezade's survival, is echoed in the

framing devices in *Midnight's Children*, *Shame* and *Haroun and the Sea of Stories.* One of the chief protagonists of *Shame* is called Omar Khayyam Shakil – he is named, in other words, after a Persian poet whose work was made famous in the West by the translations of Edward Fitzgerald. English literature, in Rushdie's hands, is far more than 'English'.

KEYWORDS

Framing device: a way of structuring stories using repeated points of reference (such as reminders that a story is being told) which are not part of the story itself, but hold it in place.

Aesthetics: the ways in which a work of art conveys its beauty and emotional content.

Rushdie also distances himself from the self-importance of the category 'literature' by taking popular culture as core to his work. He questions the literary novel's assumptions about class and taste by relating strongly to the popular culture of lived experience. The rock music world forms the background to *The Ground Beneath Her Feet*, and along the way Rushdie presents a comprehensive knowledge of the history of rock, of the technical and financial aspects of the ways in which songs are recorded and sold, and of the **aesthetics** of the music. Films such as Bollywood action movies, Disney cartoons or Hollywood classics such as *The Wizard of Oz* crop up regularly in his

One of Rushdie's sources of inspiration, *The Thousand and One Nights.* Scheherezade entertains Caliph Haroun-al-Rashid.

characters' interpretations of the worlds around them. 'Who can forget the immortal Harpo and his infant brothers in *A Day at the Races*?' the narrator asks, referring to a Marx Brothers film, in the course of describing an episode in *The Ground Beneath Her Feet* (ch. 5).

'Chekov and Zulu', one of the most powerful stories in *East, West*, explores the political fallout of the assassination of Mrs Gandhi (who was killed by her own Sikh bodyguards after she had authorised an attack on their religion's holiest shrine, the Golden Temple in Amritsar). Two old friends, both working for the Indian government, have since childhood shared a moral code based on the characters and actions of the 1960s television series *Star Trek*. Identifying with two of the series' non-American characters, they call each other Chekov and Zulu (a mis-hearing of Sulu). 'Zulu', who has been forced to confront his identity as a Sikh while trying to bring those who planned the assassination to justice, announces his departure from this code – and from the friendship with 'Chekov', and from the service of the Indian government – by referring to another fictional work, the battle between good and evil represented in J.R.R. Tolkien's epic novel *The Lord of The Rings*. 'Chekov', though, interprets his world to the last through *Star Trek* imagery.

This blending of popular and literary culture is one aspect of 'postmodernism', which has seen the renegotiation of cultural value. We no longer think a work of art is good simply because it is a painting in oils or a symphony, or bad because it is a comic illustration or a pop song. In all his work Rushdie knowledgeably and enthusiastically uses 'high' and 'popular' cultures alike, referring to the contents and echoing the techniques of past and present cultural forms through affectionate pastiche rather than bitter **parody**. Despite his obvious affection for the 'high' literatures of Britain and India, Rushdie writes beyond those high/popular boundaries – as Shakespeare or Dickens did before him.

KEYWORD

Parody: a copy which deliberately exaggerates aspects of a work, or a technique or style, usually for comic or satirical effect. See also **pastiche**.

The results are writings which refer knowingly to a kaleidoscope of other texts, continually mixing East with West, high with popular, and old with new.

BEYOND THE BOUNDARIES OF THE REAL

Rushdie also writes beyond the chief boundary of the nineteenth-century novel, **realism**. This is another aspect of postmodernism: playing with the 'real' past and present, and making an enchanted world. There are many antecedents to this tendency, and it is worth mentioning two which are important to Rushdie. J.R.R. Tolkien produced richly imagined alternative worlds based on his knowledge of the real languages and literatures of the peoples of Northern Europe, and his most accessible long work *The Lord of the Rings* was very popular with people of Rushdie's generation, who came of age in the late 1960s. Also at that moment an important Latin American novel, *One Hundred Years of Solitude*, by Gabriel Garcia Marquez, was published. It quickly became one of the standard texts of what was called 'magic realism' – a form of the novel in which extraordinary people and events are described as if they were normal, everyday. This technique was a major influence on Angela Carter, an important English novelist whose work has in turn influenced Rushdie. You can read some of his thoughts on both Marquez and another magic realist, Mario Vargas Llosa, in *Imaginary Homelands*. Rushdie bends the boundaries of realism in many ways. His principal characters are often given deformed bodies (Moraes Zogoiby's club hand, Saleem Sinai's nose, or even Neela Mahendra's extraordinary beauty, so head-turning it causes accidents). They can experience space and time in equally abnormal ways (think of the 'immortal' Flapping Eagle in *Grimus*, of Moraes Zogoiby's double-speed life, Sufiya Zinobia's shame-induced

KEYWORD

Realism: fiction which tries to be accurate in representing real places and times, and above all people who *could* be real – e.g. Mr Large, of Acacia Avenue, Wisbech. Realist characters are different from those depicted in fairy and folk tales and fantasy, who are usually there because of one characteristic which points to the moral of the story – e.g. Giant Despair of Castle Doubt.

rages, or Ormus Cama's rapid decline into premature old age). This is realism extended and distorted beyond the everyday – as we think we witness it, at least. But again, while this is partly due to Marquez, it is also influenced by Marvel – Rushdie also enthusiastically acknowledges his debt to the superhero comics which became popular in the USA in the 1930s and have spread worldwide since then. Saleem Sinai and Moraes Zogoiby are in their (inefficient) way superheroes; Moraes Zogoiby refers several times to comics' influence on his own identity.

OTHER VOICES, OTHER TIMES

Nonetheless, the basis of Rushdie's fiction *is* in the portrayal of the real. There are two aspects to this. First, his work exists in dialogue with history. Here, too, the point is not to reproduce the routine ways in which history is told, but to re-create it from a variety of perspectives. Both *Midnight's Children* and *The Ground Beneath Her Feet* emphasise the historic presence of the British in India in ways which many of the books' Indian readers found uncomfortable. *The Moor's Last Sigh* performs a similar act of historical rehabilitation for the native Christians and the Cochin Jews in Bombay. *Shame* plays a rather different game. By setting up his text within a fairy-story frame and then using the **Hegiran calendar** (dating from the time of the establishment of Islam), Rushdie is able to present us with what he calls a 'medieval' version of Pakistan. But then he takes us through what are clearly the real historical events of Pakistan's formation and subsequent history – events he has already dealt with from a different perspective in *Midnight's Children.* Through such relationships among the novels the reader of all Rushdie's fiction can compare different views of the same events such as the State of Emergency in India under Mrs Gandhi, or of the historical development of Bombay, which is the setting for all or part of *Midnight's Children*, *The Moor's Last Sigh*, and *The Ground Beneath Her Feet.* Retold in this way, from a variety of perspectives, history becomes a kaleidoscope of stories (some of which are partially or falsely remembered) rather than a single, authoritative, monolithic narrative. As Saleem Sinai puts it in *Midnight's Children:*

'I am trying to stop being mystifying. I am trying to concentrate on good hard facts. But which facts?' (book two, 'How Saleem Achieved Purity'). For Rushdie's characters, history is remembered, often inaccurately. In dealing in this way with history, Rushdie again adopts a postmodern position: for him the kaleidoscope, not the single view of orthodox 'realism', *is* the real.

KEY FACT

Hegiran calendar: The calendar of the Islamic religion starts from the point at which the Prophet Muhammad fled from Mecca to Medina, an escape known as the Hegira. In the Calendar used by the West (the Gregorian) this was in 622 AD. However, conversion between the two is not straightforward. The Hegiran calendar is based on the lunar cycle (each month starts with the new moon), and it has a different system of leap years. Rushdie uses the Hegiran calendar in *Shame* to suggest that Pakistan is both modern and living in the Middle Ages.

Second, Rushdie's work offers an equally kaleidoscopic view of the present. Here we notice the way in which Rushdie finds a unique tone of voice or accent for each of his principal characters. The technical term for this is '**idiolect**'. Dickens did this with great success. In *Hard Times* for example, he gives us Thomas Gradgrind (a rational educational reformer), who talks as if in written prose:

KEYWORD

Idiolect: a technique through which characters' individuality is shown by personalising the ways in which their speech is represented.

> I have systematically devoted myself (as you know) to the education of the reason of my family. The reason is (as you know) the only faculty to which education should be addressed.

Meanwhile Josiah Bounderby (a corrupt businessman), whatever the topic of conversation, returns to his own poor start in life. He replies to Gradgrind on this occasion:

> In idle imagination, Gradgrind … A very bad thing for anybody, but a cursed bad thing for a girl like Louisa. I should ask Mrs Gradgrind's pardon for strong expression, but that she knows very well I am not a refined character. Whoever expects refinement in *me* will be disappointed. I hadn't a refined bringing up. (C. Dickens, *Hard Times*, 1854, edition used published by Chapman & Hall, n.d., p.28)

Each of Rushdie's major characters has their own pattern of reported speech. Here, for instance, is Aurora Zogoiby in full flow in *The Moor's Last Sigh*:

> I took one look at your Bad Son, Biju, and I thought, O boy, what a handsome guy – too much sizzle, too much chilli, bring water. He may be a thief and a bounder, but that is some A-class loverboy goods. (ch. 9)

Or here is Raza Hyder at a moment of family crisis in *Shame*:

> 'I will not tell you what I think of you', Raza Hyder roars into his mouthpiece, 'but get your hide here tomorrow and take this no-good female off my hands. Not one paisa of dowry and keep out of my sight for ever after.' (ch. 8)

In both Dickens and Rushdie the effects are simultaneously comic and serious. The different grammars and spelt-out pronunciations help to show us a present which is not uniformly experienced, but seen and understood differently by the different characters. The result can be not only differences of opinion but culture clash and even crises of personal identity. In the most complex of Rushdie's novels, *The Satanic Verses*, these differences are the cause of mental breakdown. Gibreel Farishta and Saladin Chamcha each experience the present and the past as crisis – partly because their ways of seeing and expressing themselves cannot fit into others' reality (especially into the realities of Mrs Thatcher's Britain). The cumulative effect in this particular novel is a pessimistic magic realism, acknowledging the difficulties of achieving an agreed multiculturalism, and actually prefiguring the hostile ways in which many of the readers of the novel reacted to the book and its author.

OTHER BODIES, OTHER MINDS

So the Rushdie *style* is actually a *theme*, which explores the troubled relationship between what is usually agreed to be 'reality' and the personal identity of the individual. Rushdie emphasises the extraordinary in everyone: a proposal that all human life is different and each life is in its way sacred. To do this he gives his principal characters extraordinary characteristics. Many of them are physically deformed but, as we have noticed, these are not merely crippling marks but give their possessors a form of superpower. Saleem Sinai's enormous nose is useful first telepathically and then for its heightened sense of smell. Moraes Zogoiby's club hand makes him a great boxer, but he lives life at twice the normal speed, maturing sexually and attaining young manhood as a 10-year-old. Ormus Cama's brother cannot speak because of an accident at a cricket match, but he awakens Cama's own musical gifts – though his abilities are only fully realised after he lies in a coma after a car crash. He is awakened by Vina Apsara, his true love. Cama damages his hearing by performing loud rock music; he ages very quickly when Vina dies. At least in the meanwhile he has been a world-class rock musician, one of the superheroes of the late twentieth century. The transformations of Gibreel Farishta and Saladin Chamcha into devil and angel respectively, however, do not confer superpowers (though Gibreel fantasises that they do): instead they take them out of genuine contact with the real world, and enhance their mental collapse.

In this way, by emphasising the ordinariness of the extraordinary, Salman Rushdie points to the fragility of contemporary identity. We all emerge, he seems to say, from the sea of stories, each weaving our own story from the many strands of fantasy and reality which constantly surround us. We are not 'normal'; we can not take identity for granted. But in one way Rushdie's presentation of the troubles of identity follow a more orthodox path, as he reflects on the importance of family relationships to the growth of the individual. Father–son relationships are important to *Midnight's Children, The Moor's Last Sigh* and *Fury.*

Throughout his fiction there is frequent reference to the relationships between male characters and their mothers. As with the brother–sister relationship in *Grimus* and one father–daughter relationship in *Fury*, mother–son relationships often border on the incestuous. In *Midnight's Children*, Saleem's nose gains its magical telepathic ability while he is hiding and watching his mother masturbate. The novel makes several very ambivalent references to 'Mother India', as a metaphor for a country which is at the same time loved, and both loves and rejects Saleem's specialness. *Shame* is framed by the story of the three Shakil sisters, who produce Omar Khayyam Shakil in an apparently collective act, and then behave as if they were each his mother. Moraes Zogoiby, in *The Moor's Last Sigh*, lives in a turmoil of repressed desire for his mother, Aurora – and her paintings of him express that desire. Though in a more apparently innocent setting, *Haroun and the Sea of Stories* is also about the loss and return of the mother, and the quest of the two male characters to get her back. Rushdie's fictional mothers are lost and mourned, desired and feared.

In most of Rushdie's fiction there is another, more nostalgic, yearning for a past relationship. *Midnight's Children*, *The Satanic Verses*, *The Moor's Last Sigh* and *The Ground Beneath Her Feet* all explore reality and fantasy in Bombay, which is a common 'hero' in many of the stories. This great, hot, wealthy and poverty-stricken, overdeveloped and polluted city is part of Salman Rushdie's own life, and his texts portray it with a thorough and detailed nostalgia for something which has been lost for ever. The Bombay Rushdie deals with quite literally no longer exists. In *The Moor's Last Sigh*, through the character Raman Fielding, we meet the new politics of Hindu nationalism which have renamed Bombay 'Mumbai' in an attempt to erase both the British colonial past and its forebear, the Mughal empire. Otherwise, Rushdie's multicultural politics will not allow him to use the word 'Mumbai' (which is currently the city's official name). 'Bombay' is the imagined site of the potential India which did not, actually, emerge after the British had left (thanks, as Rushdie sees it, to the formation of Pakistan and the oppressive rule of Mrs Indira Gandhi). But as Rushdie's characters grow in or return to Bombay they try to make the magic work, as we see from this passage early in *The Ground Beneath Her Feet*:

> She [Vina Apsara] could prattle on in Bombay's garbage argot, *Mumbai ki kachrapati baat-cheet*, in which a sentence could begin in one language, swoop through a second, and even a third and then swing back to the first. Our acronymic name for it was *Hug-me*. Hindi Urdu Gujarati Marathi English. Bombayites like me were people who spoke five languages badly and no language well. (ch. 1)

This is no Tower of Babel, in which a many-tongued world is confused and confusing. It is a city in which the constant contact of different peoples produces a new and **hybrid** sense of being, and new energies and cultural forms are produced. But in *The Satanic Verses*, *The Ground Beneath Her Feet* and *Fury* these transformative powers are also given to the great multicultural cities of the West – to London and New York. Bombay is now part of a world in which such cities are connected by a global popular culture, by the large-scale worldwide movement of populations, by flight paths, video shops and the information superhighway. Through these chains of connection Bombay has made its presence felt in the world, and that is a part of the magic of our reality.

KEYWORD

Hybrid: produced from contact between different ethnic, religious or cultural groups, the hybrid is not just an amalgam, but – as Rushdie sees it – something new.

SALMAN AND THE SEA OF STORIES

Drawing from many different literatures, invoking a magical sense of space and time, blending history and fantasy, and delineating characters with exaggerated physical attributes and pronounced individual voices, Rushdie makes a series of interlocking parallel worlds. All this adds up to Rushdie's personal fictional voice. Here, in a passage from *Midnight's Children*, we can see the author at work, typically weaving anew from the sea of stories, from classical Greek and

Hindu myth, from Shakespeare and American film – and producing his own highly individual accent in the process:

> Once upon a time there were Radha and Krishna, and Rama and Sita, and Laila and Majnu; also (because we are not unaffected by the West) Romeo and Juliet, and Spencer Tracy and Katharine Hepburn. The world is full of love stories, and all lovers are in a sense the avatars of their predecessors. When Lila drove her Hindustan to an address off Colaba Causeway, she was Juliet coming out on to her balcony; when cream-scarfed, gold-shaded Homi sped off to meet her (in the same Studebaker in which my mother had once been rushed to Dr Narlikar's Nursing Home), he was Leander swimming the Hellespont towards Hero's burning candle. (book two, 'Commander Sabartami's Baton')

Nonetheless there is more to Rushdie's voice than this clever and knowledgeable rewriting of available tales. Rushdie's voice is personal, but it is also political, and the next chapter explores this more closely by examining his non-fictional writings.

* * * *SUMMARY* * * *

Rushdie's work established his postcolonial voice, principally by changing 'English literature' to include:

- **fantasy, myth and folk tale**
- **techniques from Bollywood film**
- **oral storytelling methods such as first-person narrators who dialogue with the listener**
- **magic realism**
- **the use of Western popular culture such as comics and rock music to signify that there is no 'East' which has not been influenced by the West.**

This makes literature a different, much more inclusive, category.

5 Major works (2): The non-fiction writing

In the aftermath of the success of *Midnight's Children*, Rushdie was quickly established as a 'writer'. This means someone who gains most of their living from writing, whose opinions are regularly sought by the media and who writes in many genres other than fiction. The 'writer' is, in other words, a public intellectual. In the early 1980s Rushdie became a 'writer' in this sense – he worked regularly as public speaker, book and film reviewer and journalist. As one of the success stories of Britain's immigrant population he was often called on by the British Council – a department of government which promotes Britain abroad – to discuss the new literary voices which were emerging in Britain and India. He was also seen by many of those immigrants as an important spokesperson, an influential voice who could represent them and their troubles in a society which was often hostile to them. This is a difficult position – the 'burden of representation' lay heavily on the shoulders of one who wished to be seen not as a British Asian voice guarding certain cultural traditions but as an individual whose identity was as much influenced by Western as Indian culture. Nonetheless, he was also aware of the problems of living as a non-white person in a racist society, and Rushdie regularly performed this representative role in the early 1980s.

THE NEW EMPIRE

In this regard the 1982 lecture 'The New Empire Within Britain' is among his most important works. It was a talk given on Channel 4, then a new television channel whose brief was quite specifically to represent members of the community not catered for by the existing channels. The talk was videotaped, and widely used by official organisations such as the Commission for Racial Equality. The talk claims that British racism (including **stereotypes** about lazy blacks or hard-working Asians) is a direct result of the 400 years or so of empire. Manifest human injustices such as slavery and indentured labour had been 'justified' at various historical moments by religious beliefs and scientific theories which sought to divide the world into good, or highly evolved (white) and less good or less highly evolved (non-white) peoples.

KEYWORD

Stereotype: a way of representing a group of people by assuming because they share one attribute, such as skin colour or place of origin, that they all share other characteristics (e.g. 'all Scots are tight with money').

The Conservative government of the time, Rushdie argued, reproduced these assumptions by characterising Britishness as a patriotic spirit which did not include non-white people. They did not, it seems, 'belong'. In fact, Rushdie reminded the viewer, that the Commonwealth immigrants who had arrived during the 1950s had been invited by a government and businesses which desperately needed them to work, and their children were no longer 'immigrants' but British citizens with no other 'home'. But they were treated by the authorities as a problem, a 'new empire within Britain'. He finishes angrily:

> The members of the new colony have only one problem, and that problem is white people. British racism, of course, is not our problem. It's yours. We simply suffer from the effects of your problem … And until you, the whites, see that the issue is not integration, or harmony, or multiculturalism, or immigration, but simply the business of facing up to and eradicating the prejudices within almost all of you, the citizens of your new, and last, Empire will be obliged to struggle against you. (*Imaginary Homelands*, p.138)

Rushdie's views offended many (white) British politicians and journalists, who tend to regard themselves as socially tolerant even when they are politically Conservative. Yet the talk was given at a time when the 'struggle' Rushdie referred to was obvious. Public unrest over the policing of areas with large immigrant communities had led to serious rioting in Brixton in South London, and Toxteth in Liverpool, in the summer of 1982. Conservatives and police chiefs were, precisely, using the language of 'problem', and they did not like the way in which Rushdie had thrown it back in their faces. One response was to characterise Rushdie as a typical public intellectual, a fairly wealthy north Londoner with friends much like himself but little or no contact with the people and problems he had described.

WRITING ROUND THE WORLD

In 1987 Salman Rushdie produced a book which reinforced the perception that he was a pampered left-wing intellectual. *The Jaguar Smile. A Nicaraguan Journey* was his first attempt at one of the staple forms of the 'writer's' craft, travel writing. This is not an unusual career step for novelists. Many of his forebears in the 'English literature' tradition were also travel writers. Take three examples from the middle of the nineteenth century: Dickens wrote a travel book, *American Notes*, which was mildly critical of some of the Americans' habits – and so it was controversial in the USA. One of Thackeray's early book-length publications, the witty *Notes on a Journey from Cornhill to Grand Cairo*, explores the impact of the European political and economic empires on the Islamic world of the Mediterranean Sea and North Africa. Anthony Trollope, meanwhile, as well as writing 47 novels and working full-time for the Post Office, managed to find the time to write long books about North America, South Africa and Australia, and a shorter one about a sea voyage to Iceland.

Partly because of this investment of time and energy by gifted novelists, travel writing has been a popular genre since the nineteenth century. But in the twentieth century its place became increasingly complex and ambivalent. Nineteenth-century Western travellers reported back to the West on experiences most of their readers could not obtain (because of the costs and time of travel). In doing so, they often caricatured and distorted what they found, making little attempt to come to terms with cultures and values which were different from their own, and convincing themselves and their readers of their own superiority to what they saw as exotic and primitive Others. In the late twentieth century, by contrast, Western travel writers were reporting back to readers most of whom could, if they wished, hop on to an aircraft and experience for themselves what the writer had reported. Meanwhile the discourse of superiority was often replaced by its opposite. Western civilisation was represented as brutal, stressful and dehumanising, while the Others were seen as repositories of an authentic, spiritualised humanity, in touch with nature. In order to make this distinction with conviction, some travel writers began to think of themselves not as tourists, looking in from the outside, but 'travellers', ready to engage with whatever they found on its own terms, and present it sympathetically.

Bruce Chatwin was one such traveller-writer. Rushdie's admiration of Chatwin is clear from the tribute essays to be found in *Imaginary Homelands.* They had journeyed together in Australia in 1984, and this journey can be seen as Rushdie's apprenticeship for *The Jaguar Smile.* Chatwin had preceded him to Latin America, producing *In Patagonia* in 1977. And yet Rushdie in Nicaragua cannot be like Bruce Chatwin in Patagonia, cannot enter into the here-or-there representations which even that complex man produced. Rushdie's own identity at this point was that of a very unorthodox Westerner, an Indo-Anglian, London-based public intellectual. He could not simply 'report back', either positively or negatively, in the ways which most travel writers do. There is more of him 'there'.

This is partly because in the 1980s Britain underwent a reinvention under the leadership of Margaret Thatcher, who interpreted the nation's internal political divisions, ambivalence about Europe, and fawning relationship with the USA, as the new national pride referred to in Rushdie's 'New Empire' talk. She set about building on this imagined unity by increasing the role of private businesses and individuals at the expense of public services and values held in common (this is the Britain portrayed critically in *The Satanic Verses*, on which Rushdie was working at the time of his Nicaraguan journey). Many British citizens, reacting to this reinvented patriotism with horror, looked elsewhere for model societies, and they wholeheartedly supported Nicaragua, a central American country ruled over by an elected socialist party called the Sandinistas (who in turn were opposed by a CIA-funded army, the Contras, in a civil war). Rushdie's journey, then, is a political one. He wants to experience a socialist utopia.

So he pursues the agenda of the late twentieth-century travel writer, looking for a society 'there' which is better than the one 'here' thanks to its authentic values. In fact, though he is sympathetic to the end, and he is deeply critical of the American and British response to the Sandinistas, he is honest enough to acknowledge that he does not find it: Nicaragua is not, yet, utopia. But he also wants to encounter something magical, mysterious, exotic – and he does. The key difference between this and other travel writing looking for paradise is that there is a *literary* magic in Latin America, the 'magic realism' of Marquez, Llosa and others which is so important to his own writing. He experiences Nicaragua through this magic. Noticing the strange mixture of shops in one town, he remarks: 'I remembered the Street of Turks in *One Hundred Years of Solitude.* In Matagalpa, Macondo did not seem so very far away' (p.7). The aesthetic strategies of writing and the politics of writing are always, simultaneously, important in Rushdie's work, and they are as important in this short book as elsewhere in his output.

Needless to say, *The Jaguar Smile* had a controversial life of its own. In fact, for all the anger raised in some quarters by *Midnight's Children* and *Shame*, or by the talk on the 'New Empire', this little travel book was the most controversial item Rushdie had yet published. As Dickens had found in the 1840s, Americans do not take criticism lightly, and Rushdie was accused of being a communist. Then as now this was a profound insult in the USA. Meanwhile in the UK the book's support of the Sandinista regime cemented his public persona as a left-wing, chattering-class intellectual out of touch with the positive events which were transforming Britain. At the time of the book's publication there was a booming stock market and rising house prices, as Britons realised that the Thatcherite attack on 'the establishment' of public services and trade unions had not, in fact, brought the world to an end. This brief moment of 'feel-good' Britain, presided over by the Conservatives, was the world into which *The Satanic Verses*, with its gloomy view of Britain as a decaying, racist state, was launched.

REPRESENTING RACE

At about this moment – 1987 – Rushdie reviewed *Handsworth Songs*, a documentary film made by black British filmmakers in and about Handsworth, a troubled inner city area of Birmingham which was the site of riots during the 1980s. Rushdie responded sympathetically but critically, saying that it was all too easy to take a **politically correct** stance on 'race' by using the official language of the university sociology department. But this jargon, he said, obscured or denied the languages of the people in the area itself. There were, he asserted, many stories to tell, including those of Handsworth residents from India and Vietnam, and in order to tell them you had to find the right language, one which must have something to do with the words of the people themselves. Referring with approval to the African American writers Maya Angelou and Toni Morrison, whose work always attempts to find the appropriate voice, Rushdie insisted that the absence of that language had marred *Handsworth Songs*, which could otherwise have told those many stories, insisting on they and their tellers' place as part of contemporary England.

KEYWORD

Politically correct: language which does not contain racial or gender prejudice – e.g. 'camera operator' instead of 'cameraman'.

This typically controversial review tells us something very important about Salman Rushdie's personal politics. It echoes the English

Romantic poet Shelley's phrase that poets are 'the unacknowledged legislators of the world'. By referring to novelists Angelou and Morrison, and criticising academic sociology, he is asserting the importance of creative writing (rather than documentary) in representing experience. To put it crudely, he is telling us that what *he* does best – writing novels – is politically important. In order to represent people, their experiences and communities, language has to be appropriate. If we all live in imaginary homelands now, then we all desperately need our stories to be woven into the general story. If the ways in which, for instance, black British people imagine themselves are denied by official public discourse (including the languages used by people who make film and television programmes, or who write reports from sociology departments, or received versions of creative writing such as the tradition of English literature), then they will always be marginalised, and the problems Rushdie identified in his 1982 talk on the inner empire will remain. It is one of the most positive signs of the remaking of Britain since that review was written that writers such as Zadie Smith and Meera Syal have indeed begun to weave new creative voices into the pattern of public discourse, and their success indicates that this kind of writing, and the place of the people it represents, is no longer marginal.

IMAGINARY HOMELANDS

You will find the *Handsworth Songs* review, and the talk on empire, in *Imaginary Homelands*, a collection of Rushdie's reprinted non-fictional material which was published in 1991. *Imaginary Homelands* seems at first sight to be a disparate collection, ranging from book reviews to political articles. As you would expect, some of it now looks rather old-fashioned or of its time. But taken together the collection has a great deal to offer the student of Salman Rushdie's work. Almost all of the book reflects on the components of the **imagined community**, and the place of creative

KEYWORD

Imagined community: the way in which we relate to large numbers of people we cannot actually know, such as the nation, is to imagine ourselves to share beliefs and ways of life.

work in making it. The opening section contains three commentaries on the writing of *Midnight's Children.* Rushdie provides many clues to his work in general, discussing for example the interweaving roles of personal memory and official history, and recounting his own efforts to remember the Bombay of his childhood. In the second section Rushdie writes angrily and unapologetically about the Nehru family dynasty in India (which includes Indira Gandhi and her sons Sanjay and Rajiv), exploring the family as an emergent myth which weaves elements of fact, literary realism and fantasy – like the *Mahabharata* or the other founding narratives of Hinduism, and, as he says, equally like a Delhi version of the American soap opera *Dallas.* (At the time of writing the Congress Party led by Sonia Gandhi is not in power in India, so this fabulous story has not yet come to an end.)

When reviewing the work of other writers, artists or filmmakers, similarly, Rushdie continually reflects on the relationships between the stories they tell and the 'real' of historical and contemporary experience. Here, for example, he discusses Terry Gilliam's *Brazil*, a film in a category all of its own (a 'paranoid political fantasy comedy' is about right) which owes something to George Orwell and Franz Kafka, and at least as much to the experience of living in Thatcher's Britain as an immigrant (Gilliam is Canadian):

> Migrants must, of necessity, make a new imaginative relationship with the world, because of the loss of familiar habitats. And for the plural, hybrid, metropolitan result of such imaginings, the cinema, in which peculiar fusions have always been legitimate … may well be the ideal location … I should add that the location of *Brazil* is a land of make-believe of which all of us who have, for whatever reason, lost a country and ended up elsewhere, are the true citizens. Like Terry Gilliam, I am a Brazilian. (*Imaginary Homelands*, p.125)

Similarly, in his brief 1992 guide to *The Wizard of Oz*, Rushdie takes exception to the end of the film, in which Dorothy returns to the grey and bleak Kansas home from which she had escaped into the colourful world of Oz, and says 'there's no place like home'. For him, the point of the story is – again – that there *is* no place, anywhere, like 'home'; the film is about migrancy, diaspora and the citizenship of the land of make believe.

So the recurrent themes of Rushdie's non-fiction match those of the novels. The reviews and essays of *Imaginary Homelands* weave pessimistic accounts of actual political corruption and failure with optimistic views of the potential cultural transformation of the world into a migrant-friendly metropolis. The starker political writing in Rushdie's non-fiction helps us to understand the political content of the fiction. Reflecting on the complexities of race and hybridity in reviewing the Handsworth film, Rushdie's political and personal agenda is restated with force. In the end what emerges from this collection is the author's belief in the importance of the exploration of different values, cultures, ideas and stories, but the rejection of any and all of these as the absolute truth. The final section of the book, matching the opening on *Midnight's Children*, contains three reflections on the political reception of *The Satanic Verses*, and his own position following that reception. Defending his novel in 'Is Nothing Sacred', a lecture read on his behalf at London's Institute of Contemporary Arts in 1990, Rushdie located himself in the contemporary world:

> The elevation of the quest for the Grail over the Grail itself, the acceptance that all that is solid *has* melted into air, that reality and morality are not givens but imperfect human constructs, is the point from which fiction begins. This is what J.-F. Lyotard called, in 1979, *La Condition Postmoderne* (*The Postmodern Condition*). The challenge of literature is to start from this point, and still find a way of fulfilling our unaltered spiritual requirements. (*Imaginary Homelands*, p.422)

These reflections remind us that since 1989 Salman Rushdie has had a very particular experience of the relationship between creative work and the real world. One of the saddest of his non-fiction publications is the introduction to his screenplay adaptation of *Midnight's Children.* The novel has not, in fact, been transferred to the screen. In the late 1980s the BBC agreed to film the novel for television in five episodes, and after working with a few screenwriters Rushdie eventually produced a script; a director was found and a number of actors cast. But the governments of India and Sri Lanka refused to allow any location filming, and the project was abandoned. In 1999 the screenplay was published, and the preface details Rushdie's narrative of the events leading to the cancellation. Rushdie the political fantasist, the 'Brazilian', has to report the failure of the real: 'As for me, the rejection of *Midnight's Children* changed something profound in my relationship with the East. Something broke, and I'm not sure it can be mended' ('Introduction', p.12).

This sadness mirrors the more confident-seeming preface to the *Vintage Book of Indian Writing.* Presenting this anthology of writings between 1947 and 1997, Rushdie remarks that little written in this period in the other Indian languages can match up to the new writing in English by Indian writers such as Vikram Seth, Amitav Ghosh and Arundhati Roy. This deliberately controversial remark has two functions. It presents Rushdie himself as an important father-figure for this new generation (the book was launched with a party at which Rushdie was photographed surrounded by these younger writers). It also reminds us that English is at the same time an Indian language, and part of another world. Well before the problems with the filming of *Midnight's Children,* Rushdie had been ambivalent about the 'real' India. As the next chapter will show, many of his critics did not like this ambivalence.

We have noted the crucial importance in many of Rushdie's novels of Bombay, a mercantile city built by imperialist traders and inhabited by a vast number of people with their own customs, languages and religious beliefs, out of whom – and only out of whom, he sometimes seems to say – comes the best of India as he imagines it, a hybridised 'secular' community in which no one set of values is dominant, and all are constantly being reinvented. Rushdie's 'truth' is this city. Wherever he is in the world, this Bombay is his imaginary homeland, his imagined community, the ever-changing place which he wishes to inhabit and which he wishes to help bring into being through his writing. But he presents the death of this idealised cosmopolitan Bombay (and its replacement by the politically limited Mumbai), in the explosions, followed by Moraes's exile, of the closing chapters of *The Moor's Last Sigh*. In *The Ground Beneath Her Feet*, Bombay exists in order to be left, and in *Fury* it remains only as an idea; there is no place like home, and Rushdie's imagined homeland is made from the sea of stories, including the Orpheus legend. Just as much as *Haroun and the Sea of Stories*, in fact, the literature, art and film reviews in Rushdie's non-fictional writings add up to a defence of writing and the other creative arts. Rushdie was defending himself against more than the *fatwa*. The next chapter will discuss the ways in which Rushdie's critics have responded to his work.

*** *SUMMARY* ***

- **Rushdie has worked as a 'writer' as well as a novelist.**
- **His other writings help us to understand the fiction, but they are well worth reading in their own right.**
- **His writings are always:**
  - **political**
  - **controversial**
  - **aspects of his self-defence.**

6 Rushdie and the critics

THE NATURE OF CRITICISM

Criticism is important. Without it the literary world would not function as a marketplace. We encounter writers, and buy or borrow books, or we decide not to do those things, because of other peoples' critical opinions. We read about books in newspapers or magazines, or we listen to our friends as they discuss a new novel they have read. We also encounter and learn about literature through the education system, in which our teachers function as literary critics and we learn to respond critically to literature. All these forms of interaction are part of literary criticism. This chapter explores some of the ways in which critics have responded to Rushdie's work

JOURNALISM AND LITERARY CRITICISM

The type of criticism the reader will most often encounter is the book review, printed in newspapers and magazines. Book reviews are usually instant responses, written quickly just after a book has been read. But this does not mean that they have trivial effects: reviews, and reviewers, are important to any book's reputation. Positive extracts from reviews are often reprinted on book covers. The back cover of the UK paperback edition of *The Moor's Last Sigh*, for instance, features sentences from five newspaper reviews, including key words such as 'a triumph ... magnificent ... exhilaratingly inventive …' Inside the book, the first two pages are devoted to similar sentence-long extracts in its praise, five of them written by novelists. Many reviewers of novels are 'writers', novelists or aspiring novelists themselves, and almost all are journalists who live in big cities such as London and New York. In other words, most reviewers are rather like the writer, critic and urban dweller Salman Rushdie, and Rushdie also reviews other novelists' work (you can read some of his book – and film – reviews in *Imaginary Homelands*). So his fellow reviewers judge him as 'one of us', and he does so in his turn – it is no coincidence that the campaign to protect him after the *fatwa* was led by novelist Fay Weldon and playwright Harold Pinter. And they do *judge* – literary reviewers try to establish a quality-led hierarchy which is as separate as possible from commercial success.

The literary criticism we all encounter

Journalistic values

The reviews and magazines share a set of values which are used to judge new work. These values praise cleverness, youth, urbanity, wit, an assumption of liberal or left-wing values shared between writer and reader, and familiarity with popular culture. A novel which displays any or all of these attributes will be welcomed. But to attain the highest critical judgement, a novel has to take itself seriously. This can be because of its subject matter or genre. However well written, romantic fiction, detective stories or sword-and-sorcery adult fantasy will not become literary prizewinners. A novel must be 'realistic' in the sense of offering a representation of the present or past as it is or could have been lived by actual human beings. But it should also go beyond the immediate lives of the characters. However successful, a comic novel such as Helen Fielding's *Bridget Jones's Diary*, which many of its readers claim to be an accurate representation of their own lives (and which engages cleverly with the literary tradition), is not as high in the literary hierarchy as any Rushdie novel for adults. The unrelentingly comic novel is lower in the hierarchy than a 'serious' novel. Rushdie's adult novels are richly comic in episodes, but they all signal their seriousness by an engagement with history. This is one way in which the 'literary' novel has always proclaimed its serious status. Tolstoy's *War and Peace*, written in the 1850s about the Napoleonic wars which had taken place 50 years earlier, or George Eliot's *Middlemarch*, which was written in the 1860s but set in the 1830s, were valued more highly at their time of publication than the contemporary-set works of Dickens. Contemporaries thought that Thackeray's *Henry Esmond* (set in the seventeenth century) was better than his *The Newcomes*, a novel of contemporary life. Salman Rushdie's most successful novel, *Midnight's Children*, is also a historical novel. Rushdie's use of history is extremely complex. His work is never simply historically accurate and it is never simply realistic; it often uses elements of fantasy. But it is never genre fiction: elements of fable and fantasy intertwine with realist narrative and historical reference.

Literary prizes

In the literary world of the 1980s and after, points mean prizes. The success of the blend which Rushdie achieved after the apprentice work of *Grimus* led to the award of the Booker Prize for *Midnight's Children.* While the novel is undoubtedly a fine achievement, there is a problem here, which has affected Rushdie's output (and others') considerably. The literary world's attempt to produce a hierarchy based on a shared sense of literary value divorced from commercial considerations has in fact produced a type of writing which is aimed squarely at the winning of literary prizes (which usually means big sales). So there is a 'Bookerocracy' of novelists who write similar ambitious, serious historical and philosophical novels which tend to be shortlisted for literary prizes. This category of what could be called 'prize writing' has limited the expectations of writers, judges and readers alike. The comparative failure of *Shame* convinced Rushdie that he needed to write longer and more complex books, and he then arguably tried too hard to reproduce the scope of *Midnight's Children*. This is something which he has promised to stop – he has claimed that his future novels will be compact and to the point, more like *Fury* than its predecessor, *The Ground Beneath Her Feet*; it will be interesting to see whether these works have any effect on the Booker Prize itself.

ACADEMIC LITERARY CRITICISM

The reader will find academic literary criticism at school, or through any university course in literature, or by searching in the press, in bookshops and on the Internet. Academic criticism is unlike the book review chiefly because it is written more slowly, carefully and reflectively. It is much more extensive in its use of comparison, and it is usually explicitly theoretical and political. It can therefore help us to understand Rushdie's work in ways which the quickly written review cannot. However, it is not neutrally helpful. Though academics are often metropolitan intellectuals themselves, unlike journalists they do not see Salman Rushdie as 'one of them'. Most of them are not novelists or aspiring novelists, but professional critics who value literary theory at least as much as the fiction and poetry they criticise. However, society as a whole values 'creativity' more highly than 'theory', and academic literary criticism which uses 'theory' to judge 'creativity' can raise issues which obscure the pleasures which most of us take from reading. This tendency is reinforced when academics consider contemporary fiction from a political standpoint, as we shall see.

Like the reviewers, academic judges also produce a literary hierarchy, and though this has little to do with the simple mechanics of prizes and sales, it is also important to a book's success. Academic study puts books on to the curriculum, and students buy books – this is also, in other words, a form of marketing. Academic literary theory values complexity, technical sophistication, familiarity with the traditions of high (and sometimes popular) culture, and informed critical and political engagement. Academic critics prefer that the writer should be aware of her/his own position and of the context of literary tradition(s) and contemporary cultural production, and should produce work which enables the critic to engage with that awareness. Few academic critics today are openly concerned with hierarchies of quality – in other words, they claim not to be interested in whether or why one writer might be 'better' than another (though in fact most of the writers they study, whether contemporary or from the past, are by common agreement high-quality writers).

RUSHDIE'S PLACE IN LITERATURE

Before looking at Salman Rushdie's work, the academic critic must answer a big question: how, if at all, does Rushdie fit into 'English literature'? Perhaps the best answer is that he has reinvented it. This is not a question of birth or nationality – Rushdie has had a British passport since the 1960s, and anyway writers in English such as the American, Henry James, and the Pole, Joseph Conrad, have been taught as part of 'English Literature' for the past century. Rushdie's work is mostly set on the Indian subcontinent (as was most of Kipling's). He has himself refused the category 'Commonwealth literature', and insisted that 'literature in English' is the category he wishes to belong to – a position he reinforced in his preface to the *Vintage Book of Indian Writing*. So here we have a new, multi-layered category which refuses one orthodoxy while trying to establish another, and it is no surprise to find Rushdie considered in surveys as different as Sara Suleri's *The Rhetoric of English India* (which sees him as, if problematically, 'Indian') and Steven Connor's *The English Novel in History 1950–1995* (which sees him as, equally problematically, 'English'). Of course Rushdie is part of English literature in the important sense that he uses it all the time in his own writing. In other words, he makes his own work part of the tradition which he is reinventing. Damian Grant's 1999 examination of Rushdie's work points out some of the ways in which he uses the work of eighteenth-century English literature writers such as Swift, Defoe, Sterne and Fielding, and we have seen here how he also draws from later writers such as Dickens or Joyce. In the latter, of course, we face a similar problem: the ambivalent place of Irish writers in 'English literature' underlines the point that Rushdie has made many times. The category has to do with languages and traditions, but not with political or legal structures. In the twenty-first century, 'English' has to be seen as a language and tradition, but not a location.

RUSHDIE AS A POSTMODERNIST?

The critic must also ask whether Rushdie fits into any existing category of writing. The complexity of design in the novels, and the use of the literary tradition to reinvent their language, might indicate that Rushdie is a 'modernist', like Joyce or Virginia Woolf – someone for whom the manipulation of language has become more important than generating realist representations of life. If so, this might be because the writer is comfortably placed as a Western intellectual, and can indulge in experiment, whereas oppressed people still have an urgent need to represent their conditions using realist techniques. Indeed, this claim has been made by Aijaz Ahmad, who accuses Rushdie, in *Shame* in particular, of playing amusing games with the histories and nation-states of South Asia. Ahmad, though, is not amused. This might be fun for Rushdie and his Western readers, Ahmad says, but it denies the possibilities of liberation from within those states by denying the voices and imaginations of the people who live there. (This is, of course, precisely Rushdie's criticism of the film *Handsworth Songs.*) As Ahmad sees it, Rushdie is at best a patronising Westerner divorced from reality, and therefore a bad writer because his Westernised writing, in English, is part of the new imperialism of global capital, which has no time for the authentic voices of the developing world.

However, the casual use of fantasy drawn from the world's sea of stories, the parallel worlds in space and time, the debt to Bollywood film technique, and the pervasive use of popular culture as reference points, indicates that Rushdie has journeyed beyond the careful elitism of the Westernised literary modernist, and into 'postmodernism'. Most critics accept that Rushdie is a postmodern writer (though they do not all approve). But he is, as we have seen, a postmodern writer who insists on the importance of hybridity as the crucible for the emergence of the new, and who makes no claim to defend authentic traditions, however aware of them he might be. His ideal form of life is the flux of identity in the big postcolonial cities such as Bombay and London, which as he sees it have destabilised any sense of what could be meant by 'Western' superiority. From this point of view Aijaz Ahmad's argument is unsustainable. In other words, *Shame* has to be read alongside *The Ground Beneath Her Feet* – in which Rushdie uses a postmodern sense of the unreliability of history and memory to demonstrate that the reinvention of memory, history, myth and identity is a process which the West cannot control.

A writer's viewpoint

If we agree that much of the coverage of *The Satanic Verses* is purely political, and has very little reference to the content of the book (which many of its opponents acknowledge that they have not read), *Shame* stands as Salman Rushdie's most controversial novel among literary academics. Despite the fairytale framing of the text, the compactness of the book leaves little hiding place for what seems to be the author's real political anger about a real place. Aijaz Ahmad and Ziauddin Sardar have produced angry responses to what they see as the novel's Westernised representation of Pakistan.

The feminist response

They have been joined in this condemnation by a number of **feminist** critics, for whom Rushdie's writing – and *Shame* in particular – reveals an attitude of hostility to women. The representation of Mrs Gandhi in *Midnight's Children* as 'Mother India' or 'the Widow' seems modelled on the destructive aspect of the Hindu Goddess Kali. With this portrayal, or with that of Moraes Zogoiby's heartless and manipulative seducer Uma Sarasvati in *The Moor's Last Sigh*, or with any of the principal female characters in *Fury*, Rushdie can be accused of dealing in negative stereotypes of women. Catherine Cundy, in her 1996 study of Rushdie's work, reviews the representation of women in the novels (*Grimus* and *Shame* in particular) and finds Rushdie wanting. Noticing his attitude both to powerful women such as Mrs Gandhi and Mrs Thatcher, and a tendency to represent female characters such as Bird-Dog in *Grimus* and Amina Sinai in *Midnight's Children* as sexually vulnerable, Cundy claims that he resents women as a whole. She concludes that 'Rushdie's self-appointed status as champion of women in the face of religious, political and cultural constraints upon their freedom cannot go unchallenged' (C. Cundy, *Salman Rushdie*, Manchester University Press, 1997, p.105).

> **KEYWORD**
>
> **Feminism:** examines gender relationships and tries to redress the imbalances of power between men and women. Feminist literary criticism examines literature from this point of view.

Rushdie as a postcolonialist

This strong, often angry criticism of Rushdie's representation of the developing world, and of its women in particular, seems to call into question the ways in which his work fits into the category 'Postcolonial'. Of course in a very simple sense Rushdie's output has to be seen as postcolonial – his work deals with contemporary India and Pakistan, and with Western cities with large populations drawn from parts of the world which emerged from Western imperial conquest during the third quarter of the twentieth century, and that is that. Postcolonial theory and literary criticism, however, attempts to play a political role and, despite his sympathies, which are obvious in the essays in *Imaginary Homelands* and in the novels themselves, Rushdie's work cannot be lined up against a wish-list of correct political positions. In particular, the project of postcolonial literature (and literary criticism) claims to allow a voice to the oppressed – people from the various former empires 'write back' against the West's attempts to impose its own voice on their histories and identities. Rushdie's personal position as a privately educated Londoner with a background in advertising would, according to his critics, deny this, as would his insistence on the importance of writing in English.

This attitude rejects all postmodern art, claiming that postmodernism's politics of identity, rather than a politics based on class or gender difference or global inequality, is in fact based on the kind of consumerism which plays into the hands of the **transnational** corporations of global capitalism. British critic Terry Eagleton refuses postmodernism any claim to political progressivism on these grounds, as does the influential critic of global capitalism, Naomi Klein. For such authors, the values of identity politics become those of lifestyle choice, including the adoption by wealthy Westerners of non-Western forms of spirituality (such as transcendental meditation, or feng shui) or diet (such as Thai or sushi cuisine). These moments of 'taste', sampled from Other cultures, are seen as marketing opportunities by transnational corporations who produce books and television programmes about them, while the people from whom the ideas and products originated receive nothing. In this view, Rushdie is part of the problem. His work displays the non-Western world for Western consumption.

KEYWORD

Transnational: many large capitalist companies are genuinely global in operation and have no national 'home'. They operate wherever they can make the most profit.

Rushdie as an Orientalist

Whatever the merits of this line of argument (and it must certainly be agreed that Rushdie's publishers are global capitalists based in the West), postcolonial criticism of this sort can only resist in the name of some authentic unchanging essence which is vulnerable to corruption by the new imperialism of lifestyle politics. Thus for writers such as Aijaz Ahmad and Ziauddin Sardar, Salman Rushdie is a typical 'Orientalist'. **Orientalism** was identified by the critic, Edward Said, who looked at the ways in which Western writers, historians, archaeologists and artists had imagined the 'East' (the mainly Islamic world beyond the Balkans) from the beginning of the nineteenth century onwards. He found a consistent portrayal of the East as decaying in power, politically corrupt and erotically available – the obsessive Western interest in the harem being the clearest signal of this attitude. The West claimed to have a superior knowledge of the East, whereas, claimed Said, what the West actually produced was merely a mirror image of its own desires. If Rushdie's work is indeed Orientalist in this sense, then it is a tissue of misrepresentations which can tell us nothing of India or Pakistan, but only something of the literary world of the West in the late twentieth century.

KEYWORDS

Orientalism: the way in which the West, convinced of its own superiority, studies and produces knowledge of the East, especially the Islamic world.

Binary oppositions: simple judgemental ways of dividing the world (us/them, black/white, good/bad), which can often embody stereotyped hostility to Others.

It should be noted that Edward Said himself, who (being a wealthy and cosmopolitan Syrian Christian who works at an American University) is more like Salman Rushdie than the average academic critic, does not agree with this angry reading of Rushdie's work; he has been one of Rushdie's defenders. There is, indeed, another sort of postcolonial criticism, to be found in the work of other denationalised intellectuals such as Homi Bhabha and Gayatri Chakravorty Spivak (both of whom are Indian in origin but work in American universities). While this type of criticism is very difficult to read, it refuses altogether the simple **binary oppositions** (such as Pakistani is good, Western is bad) which seem to motivate Aijaz Ahmad and the other opponents of Rushdie. Bhabha insists that the world is indeed postcolonial; there is no going back to some paradise of pre-imperial or pre-capitalist harmony, or of authentic cultural wholeness. This does not mean that there are no power relations in the world (he, like Rushdie, identifies various forms of pervasive racism and opposes them). However, he says, what we have to work with (and work against racism with) is the mutations and hybridities of the new urban cultures. This is precisely Rushdie's position.

KEYWORD

Binary oppositions: simple judgemental ways of dividing the world (us/them, black/white, good/bad), which can often embody stereotyped hostility to Others.

THE SUCCESSES, AND THE REST

The critical success of *Midnight's Children* across journalism and the wider literary world led to the 'establishment' of Rushdie, and to the emergence of a hybrid British-postimperial-Indian voice which has been taken up, in different ways, by writers such as Hanif Kureishi and Meera Syal. Rushdie is constantly judged by the standards of *Midnight's Children.* The 'disappointments' – *Shame, The Moor's Last Sigh* and *The Ground Beneath Her Feet* – were judged to be comparative failures by the standards of *Midnight's Children.* The least acknowledged success, on the other hand, is the excellent *Haroun and the Sea of Stories,* perhaps Rushdie's finest achievement so far, which criticism finds difficult to cope with because it is a children's book – in Damian Grant's book on Rushdie, for example, *Haroun* has only seven pages of coverage, compared with 11 for *Grimus* and 21 for *The Satanic Verses,* and its coverage in this book is also comparatively slight.

The crisis over *The Satanic Verses,* however, was rather different. *The Satanic Verses* can also claim to be Rushdie's finest work. It is certainly his most complex, ambitious and fully realised novel, its surreal twists of plot, place, time and character emerging, challenging and resolving within a formal structure which bends but never breaks. But whatever the book's literary achievement, it has of course been caught up in a more acute postcolonial crisis than anything which Aijaz Ahmad could throw at it. The book is part of a general crisis of the Western liberal intellectual, in fact, as well as part of a postimperial political crisis over the place of Islam in the contemporary world, and the Chapter 7 will reflect on Rushdie's part in this general crisis.

*** * * SUMMARY * * ***

- There are two types of criticism: short reviews, often in newspapers, and lengthier academic criticism. Each is important.
- Newspaper reviews are usually by people similar to Rushdie. They are usually positive and supportive.
- Academic reviews are more considered. They are sometimes very hostile. They ask such questions as:
  - Does Rushdie write 'English literature'?
  - Is he a postcolonial writer?
  - Is he a postmodern writer?
  - Is his work in any way feminist?

7 Reading Rushdie in the twenty-first century

THE NEW LITERARY WORLD

In this book we have come across Salman Rushdie in several guises, as a public intellectual, as a reviewer and travel writer, and as a would-be television and film writer, as well as a short story writer and novelist. In many ways it is easier to think of Rushdie under the inclusive general term 'writer' (in the ways outlined in Chapter 5) rather than 'novelist'. But whether we think of him as a public intellectual, a general-purpose writer or as a novelist, we have to see him in his time, and in the early twenty-first century the place of the writer is changing rapidly.

Novels are important products, and whether used for amusement or guides to life, they are taken seriously by a wide variety of people. But novelists themselves – even literary magicians like Rushdie – are less powerful people than they were 100 years ago. The technologies of communication, including film and television, desktop publishing and word processing, have made it easier to produce literary texts and all other forms of writing. For those with access to it (and we should remember that many in the West as well as in the developing world do not have access) the Internet has led to the democratisation of publishing and of opinion. As a result of this deluge of information there is far less common agreement about what is good, and what is not, whether in 'high' or 'popular' culture. Rushdie is well aware of this tendency. In the globally connected world which he depicts in *The Ground Beneath Her Feet* and *Fury*, the life of an academic has very little public value, and the most successful cultural products are music and sophisticated toys and games.

But the novel, and other forms of writing, do remain important. As Rushdie is well aware, language itself is *not* just a game. English continues its seemingly relentless progress as the world's second language, and the first language of business communication. It is taught as a form of communication, and this way of teaching and learning tends to standardise the language, propagating English as a relatively unchanging entity and implying that those who speak or write it differently are wrong. There is, therefore, an urgent need to read and write novels which explore and create the future of the English language, written by and expressive of all the peoples who speak it. For all the complaints of his postcolonial critics, Salman Rushdie is among the guardians of the expressive future of the language.

The idea of a common cultural authority has been weakened by these tendencies. There are several potential trends here, the first of which we have noticed in a slightly different context. Publishers want bestsellers, and they need some agreed source of authority with which to market them. One source of contemporary cultural authority is the literary prize (and its equivalent in other arts such as the Oscars, and in the UK the Turner Prize in art or the Mercury Prize in music). This tendency has already changed the ways in which novelists write (and as we have seen it has had a profound effect on Rushdie's career; the comparative failure of *Shame* led him to write *The Satanic Verses*). Potential prizewinners are, of course, publishable.

However, it is probable that the criteria for publishability will become more closely tied to the notion of 'filmability'. Many publishers are already component parts of transnational corporations, which can maximise their investments in the few products which achieve global sales success by marketing them in different formats. This is already important in the relation between successful fiction and film – Nick Hornby's *High Fidelity* and Helen Fielding's *Bridget Jones's Diary* are examples of 1990s' novels which have been filmed successfully. It is possible that this potential is one of the reasons for Salman Rushdie's change of tactics towards producing more, shorter and sharper, novels. *Fury*, chiefly set in New York and with a smaller gallery of principal characters, is, quite simply, more easily filmable than any of its predecessors; and a British or American film adaptation of this novel would not necessarily have to deal with the intense political pressures which caused the cancellation of the filming of *Midnight's Children.* Rushdie may yet become a novelist who generates screenplays; given his affection for both Bollywood and Hollywood, such a transformation might suit him well.

Is this the future of Rushdie the novelist?

THE FUTURE OF THE NOVEL

But we (and, much more to the point, Salman Rushdie) must not abandon the novel yet. Whatever the skills of special effects teams such as Industrial Light and Magic, the novel can do things which cannot be put on film or coded into video games. The complexities of multiple narrative voices, the subtle fantasies of magic realism, the historical sweep across time and the troubling eroticism of incestuous sexual desire, are all aspects of Rushdie's work which neither cinema nor television could represent without breaking its own codes almost beyond repair.

The novel emerged as a form at the same time as Western imperialism, and it became established around the world as a result of imperialism. Late imperial and postcolonial writers such as Mulk Raj Anand, R.K. Narayan, V.S. Naipaul and Anita Desai have used the novel to write back against the tyrannies which resulted from this process (such as the beginnings of the South Asian diaspora in the indentured labour of the Caribbean), and in doing so they have reinvented the novel and the concept of literature, to its great enrichment. This achievement has been transmitted onwards through Rushdie's work, and its international success. Now there is a generation of writers who have used Rushdie's techniques, and his success, in order to widen still further the representation of South Asian cultures in the English-speaking and wider world. This is in many ways his greatest achievement and, whatever he may do in the future, it will continue his work.

* * * *SUMMARY* * * *

- **New communications technology means that most people can 'publish' opinions.**
- **Publishers are parts of mass entertainment and communications corporations.**
- **Rushdie's decision to write shorter novels may have to do with the need to produce texts for different media.**
- **All his work has asked about the meaning of literature. He is now asking us about the future of the novel.**

8 Where to next?

READ RUSHDIE'S WORK

The novels are complex, and all repay several readings. As we have seen, the fiction and other writings need to be taken together if we are to understand Rushdie's work, and a reading of *Imaginary Homelands* will illuminate any of the novels. Further guidance, and a different aspect of the author's voice, can be found in the many interviews with Rushdie. The useful *Salman Rushdie Bibliography*, edited by Joel Kuortti, and published in Frankfurt by Peter Lang in 1997, lists many of these (and you will find more recent ones on the Internet) as well as many academic articles.

READ THE CRITICS

Several short studies of Rushdie's work provide helpful further discussion. The first of these (and the most critical) is Timothy Brennan's *Salman Rushdie and the Third World*, published by Macmillan in 1989; more recently we have three books entitled *Salman Rushdie.* Catherine Cundy's was published by Manchester University Press in 1997; D.C.R.A. Goonetilleke's, by Macmillan in 1998 and Damian Grant's by Northcote House in 1999. Read one or two of these before you look at the interesting but challenging book of essays, *Reading Rushdie*, edited by M.D. Fletcher, which was published by Rodopi in Amsterdam in 1994. This also contains an extensive bibliography.

Rushdie's work is already seen as an important part of the literary tradition, and you will find his novels treated seriously in a large number of surveys of recent literature. Two books which place him (ambivalently) in an 'Anglo-Indian' tradition are Sara Suleri's influential *The Rhetoric of English India*, which Chicago University Press published in 1992, and William Walsh's *Indian Literature in English*, published by Longman in 1990. Seeing Rushdie from a (slightly) more 'English literary' perspective are Steven Connor, *The English Novel in History 1950–95*, which Macmillan published in 1996, and novelist D.J. Taylor's survey *After the War: The Novel and English Society Since 1945*, published by Chatto & Windus in 1993.

Postcolonial criticism which takes Rushdie as its object, sometimes unkindly, includes Brennan's book, and Aijaz Ahmad, *In Theory. Classes, Nations, Literature*, published in 1992 by Verso. A briefer version of this negative view can be found in Ziauddin Sardar's *Cultural Studies For Beginners*, published by Icon in 1997. More generally, Edward Said's *Orientalism*, published by Penguin in 1992, and Benedict Anderson, *Imagined Communities*, published by Verso in 1983, provide insights into the ways in which knowledge and community can interact. Read those before the more difficult Homi Bhabha, *Nation and Narration*, published by Routledge in 1992.

Though Rushdie is still living incognito, the many books and articles written about *The Satanic Verses* affair now seem dated. More helpful are books exploring the ambivalent place of Islam in the modern world: Aziz Al-Azmeh, *Islams and Modernities*, published in 1993 by Verso, is a good example. The general crisis of intellectual authority referred to in Chapter 6 is discussed in a collection of essays edited by Jeremy Jennings and Anthony Kemp-Welch, *Intellectuals in Politics. From the Dreyfus Affair to Salman Rushdie*, published in 1997 by Routledge.

RUSHDIE ON THE WEB

The World Wide Web is dynamic and volatile. New sites appear, and old ones disappear, all the time. But there is always plenty of Rushdie material out there! The best thing to do is keyword searches on Salman Rushdie and the individual book titles. Most of the Internet material on Rushdie is about *The Satanic Verses*, and while this can be interesting it is usually very one-sided (whether for or against Rushdie's 'right to publish'). However, at the time of writing the best Rushdie website was in fact on *The Satanic Verses*:

http://www.wsu.edu:8080/~brians./anglophone/satanic_verses

This site, edited from Washington State University by Paul Brians, goes through the novel chapter by chapter, with a glossary of characters, and has many links to other Rushdie sites and to sites which discuss contemporary literary and cultural theory.

GLOSSARY

Aesthetics The ways in which a work of art conveys its beauty and emotional content.

Binary oppositions Simple, judgemental ways of dividing the world (us/them, black/white, good/bad), which can often embody stereotyped hostility to Others.

Classical mythology The set of myths and legends dealing with the gods and goddesses of ancient Greece and Rome.

Diaspora Originally this referred to the spread of the Jewish people round the world. The term is used to refer to any population which has dispersed as a result of imperialism – African and Irish peoples, as well as Asians.

Feminism Examines gender relationships and tries to redress the imbalances of power between men and women. Feminist literary criticism examines literature from this point of view.

Framing device A way of structuring stories using repeated points of reference (such as reminders that a story is being told) which are not part of the story itself, but hold it in place.

Hybrid Produced from contact between different ethnic, religious or cultural groups, the hybrid is not just an amalgam, but – as Rushdie sees it – something new.

Idiolect A technique through which characters' individuality is shown by personalising the ways in which their speech is represented.

Imagined community The way in which we relate to large numbers of people we cannot actually know, such as the nation, is to imagine ourselves to share beliefs and ways of life.

Magic realism A technique used first by a number of Latin American writers which describes extraordinary people and events as if they were part of normal, everyday reality.

Metanarrative An outline story repeated through many other stories. For example, boy meets girl, and they marry in the final chapter, is the metanarrative of most nineteenth-century novels. The characters are called different names, and the detail of places and events are different, but the outline of the story remains the same, whether in Charlotte Brontë's *Jane Eyre* or Charles Dickens's *Little Dorrit.*

Metaphor A form of comparison using a word or idea which is not literally applicable to what the writer is describing, in order to illustrate shared characteristics.

Modernism A movement which started in the early twentieth century. Writers, artists and musicians broke with the conventions of their art forms, producing work which was difficult to understand. It often shocked and disturbed audiences.

Multicultural Thanks to the shifting populations of the postcolonial world, many cities are inhabited by groups of people with significantly different religious and cultural systems, which do not simply integrate into one new community but evolve together, sometimes uneasily.

Oral storytelling Traditions in which stories are learned and transmitted by the spoken word rather than through writing.

Orientalism The way in which the West, convinced of its own superiority, studies and produces knowledge of the East, especially the Islamic world.

Other, the A term to help us understand that we define ourselves by defining what or who we are not. Derived from psychoanalysis, the term has become important in postcolonial theory.

Parody A copy which deliberately exaggerates aspects of a work, or a technique or style, usually for comic or satirical effect.

Pastiche A copy not of a work but of a style or technique, which tries to mimic the original as closely as possible.

Politically correct Language which does not contain offensive racial or gender prejudice – e.g. 'camera operator' instead of 'cameraman'.

Postcolonial After the European empires dissolved in the second half of the twentieth century, people in the former colonies, and those who had moved round the world as a result of the empires, found new ways of expressing themselves and coming to terms with their pasts.

Postmodernism In the second half of the twentieth century many artists rejected modernism. They used the traditions of popular culture and high art together, playfully mixing all kinds of sources. This work is usually less disturbing to audiences than modernism.

Realism Fiction which tries to be accurate in representing real places and times, and above all people who *could* be real – e.g. Mr Large, of Acacia Avenue, Wisbech. Realist characters are different from those depicted in fairy and folk tales and fantasy, who are usually there because of one characteristic which points to the moral of the story – e.g. Giant Despair of Castle Doubt.

Revelation The idea that truth is revealed to a writer by a Divine source. In the Jewish and Christian tradition, the Ten Commandments are an example. In the Muslim faith, it is believed that the truth was revealed to the Prophet Muhammad by the Angel Gabriel.

Satire A representation of public figures, or social trends, which exaggerates their worst features. Usually political, as well as comic, in intention.

Schizophrenia A mental disease in which thoughts and actions are disconnected. Schizophrenics often experience multiple personalities – they think of themselves as several different people – or they experience inner voices, which they do not think are their own, telling them what to do.

Soliloquy A speech given out loud by an individual, with no listener present. A common device used in drama and fiction to allow an audience to hear what a character is thinking.

South Asia India, Pakistan, Bangladesh and Sri Lanka. A more inclusive term than the one formerly used, the 'Indian subcontinent'.

Stereotype A way of representing a group of people by assuming because they share one attribute that they all share other characteristics (e.g. 'all Scots are tight with money').

Transnational Many large capitalist companies are genuinely global in operation and have no national 'home'. They operate wherever they can make the most profit.

Yuppie Literally 'young, upwardly mobile professional person'. The term was used satirically to describe the aggressive and selfish people who were successful in the 1980s.

Chronology of major works

1975 *Grimus*, the first novel; unsuccessful

1981 *Midnight's Children*, the first critical success, the first literary prize (the Booker Prize) and the first controversy: a passage is removed after legal action by the Nehru family

1983 *Shame* echoes the controversy in its portrayal of Pakistan, but not the prizewinning success

1987 *The Jaguar Smile. A Nicaraguan Journey* relates the author's travels in the landscape of magic realism

1988 *The Satanic Verses* stirs political controversy which results in riots, deaths and the internal exile of the author

1990 *Haroun and the Sea of Stories* combines entertainment for children with the writer's first response to his predicament

1991 *Imaginary Homelands*, a sequence of essays provides a guide and commentary on Rushdie's work so far

1992 *The Wizard of Oz*, a brief commentary on one of Rushdie's favourite, and inspirational, films, with a personal twist at the end

1994 *East, West*, a collection of stories exploring aspect of Rushdie's multiple identity

1995 *The Moor's Last Sigh*, the first full-length adult novel since *The Satanic Verses* gives another perspective on political and religious change in India, and on the writer in exile

1999 *The Ground Beneath Her Feet*, perhaps the least political full-length novel since *Grimus*, explores the relationships between myth and creativity. Screenplay version of *Midnight's Children*, published together with an account of the reasons for its non-appearance as a television series

2001 *Fury*, the briefest novel since *Shame*, appears and once again explores myth, creativity and science fiction

FURTHER READING

Ahmad, A. *In Theory. Classes, Nations, Literature*, London: Verso (1992)

Akhtar, S. *Be Careful with Muhammad! The Salman Rushdie Affair*, London: Bellew Publishing (1989)

Al-Azmeh, A. *Islams and Modernities*, London: Verso (1993)

Anderson, B. *Imagined Communities*, London: Verso (1983)

Bhabha, H. *Nation and Narration*, London: Routledge (1992)

Brennan, T. *Salman Rushdie and the Third World*, London: Macmillan (1989)

Connor, S. *The English Novel in History 1950–95*, London: Macmillan (1996)

Cundy, C. *Salman Rushdie*, Manchester: Manchester University Press (1997)

Eagleton, T. *The Illusions of Postmodernism*, Oxford: Blackwell (1996)

Fletcher, M.D. ed. *Reading Rushdie*, Amsterdam: Rodopi (1994)

Goonetilleke, D.C.R.A. *Salman Rushdie*, London: Macmillan (1998)

Grant, D. *Salman Rushdie*, London: Northcote House (1999)

Jennings, J. and A. Kemp-Welch, *Intellectuals in Politics. From the Dreyfus Affair to Salman Rushdie*, London: Routledge (1997)

Kuortti, J. *Salman Rushdie Bibliography*, Frankfurt: Peter Lang (1997)

Kureishi, H. *The Black Album*, London: Faber and Faber (1995)

Kureishi, H. *My Son the Fanatic*, London: Faber and Faber (1998)

Roy, A. *The God of Small Things*, London: Flamingo (1997)

Ruthven, M. *A Satanic Affair. Salman Rushdie and the Rage of Islam*, London: Chatto and Windus (1990)

Said, E. *Culture and Imperialism*, London: Chatto and Windus (1993)

Said, E. *Orientalism*, second edition, London: Penguin (1992)

Sardar, Z. *Cultural Studies For Beginners*, Cambridge: Icon (1997)

Seth, V. *A Suitable Boy*, London: Phoenix (1995)

Seth, V. An Equal Music, London: Phoenix (1999)

Smith, Z. White Teeth, London: Penguin (2000)

Suleri, S. *The Rhetoric of English India*, Chicago: Chicago University Press (1992)

Syal, M. *Anita and Me*, London: HarperCollins (1996)
Taylor, D.J. *After the War: The Novel and English Society Since*, Chatto & Windus (1993)
Walsh, W. *Indian Literature in English*, London: Longman (1990)

INDEX